Jonas. Trumbauer

Praise Hymns and Full Salvation Songs

Jonas. Trumbauer

Praise Hymns and Full Salvation Songs

ISBN/EAN: 9783337182045

Printed in Europe, USA, Canada, Australia, Japan

Cover: Foto ©Thomas Meinert / pixelio.de

More available books at **www.hansebooks.com**

Praise Hymns

and

Full Salvation Songs

Compiled by

Rev. Jonas Trumbauer.

Journey in the King's Highway.

Harriet E. Jones. Adam Geibel.

1. Would you go re-joicing on In the light of God's dear Son? Come and
2. Would you tread among the flow'rs, Would you rest in sylvan bow'rs? Come and
3. Would you gain a home on high In the gold-en by and by? Come and

journey in the King's highway; Would you ev'ry moment prove All the
journey in the King's highway; Would you drink from living rills Flowing
journey in the King's highway; Would you live with God's dear Son While e-

sweetness of his love? Come and journey in the King's highway.
from the E-den hills? Come and journey in the King's highway.
ter-nal years roll on? Come and journey in the King's highway.

CHORUS.

Come and jour — ney, come and jour - ney, Come and
Come and jour-ney, come and jour-ney in the King's high-way, Come and

jour — ney, come and jour - ney; Come this moment and be glad,
journey, come and journey in the King's highway;

Copyright, 1898, by J. Howard Entwisle.

Journey in the King's, etc.—CONCLUDED.

Come, in shining robes be clad, And go singing in the King's highway.

Into His Marvellous Light.

E. E. Hewitt. Jno. R. Sweney.

1. Won-derful mercy that sought us, Wand'ring a-far in the night;
2. Singing love's beauti-ful sto-ry, Ech-o the heav'nly re-frain;
3. Out from the sin and its sor-row, In-to the life pure and free;
4. Soon shall we meet by the riv-er, There in sweet songs we'll unite;

Fine.

Precious the Saviour who brought us In-to his marvellous light.
Blessing and hon-or and glo-ry Be to the Lamb that was slain.
Waiting the glo-ri-ous mor-row, When our Redeemer we'll see.
Je-sus will bring us for-ev-er In-to his marvellous light.

D.S.—Bro't from the kingdom of dark-ness In-to his marvellous light.

CHORUS. *D.S.*

Saved to the glo-ry of Je-sus! Saved by the power of his might!

Copyright, 1896, by Jno. R. Sweney. *Praise Hymns—B*

12. He Set the Joy-Bells Ringing.

E. E. Hewitt.
Jno. R. Sweney.

1. Oh, bless the Lord, he cleansed my soul, And filled my lips with singing;
2. He placed my feet up-on the Rock, The on-ly sure foundation;
3. His promise is for "all the days," His love for me is car-ing;
4. Then let me tell the hap-py news To oth-er souls around me;
5. His love is call-ing, seeking still, Come, ev-'ry burden bringing;

He came in my poor, sin-ful heart, And set the joy-bells ringing.
He shows me wonders of his grace, The blessings of sal-va-tion.
While in the "Father's House" above, A mansion he's pre-par-ing.
I'm safe within the blessed fold, For Je-sus came and found me.
The touch of Christ within your heart Will set the joy-bells ringing.

CHORUS.

Oh, praise the Lord, he first loved me, I feel new life up-springing;

He came in my poor, sin-ful heart, And set the joy-bells ringing.

Copyright, 1891, by Jno. R. Sweney.

The Cross is not Greater. 13

B. B.
Gen. BALLINGTON BOOTH.

May be sung as a Solo and Chorus.

1. The cross that he gave may be heavy, But it ne'er outweighs his grace,
2. The thorns in my path are not sharper Than composed his crown for me,
3. The light of his love shineth brighter, As it falls on paths of woe,
4. His will I have joy in ful- filling, As I'm walking in his sight,

The storm that I feared may surround me, But it ne'er excludes his face.
The cup that I drink not more bitter Than he drank in Gethsema - ne.
The toil of my work groweth lighter, As I stoop to raise the low.
My all to the blood I am bringing, It a - lone can keep me right.

CHORUS.

The cross is not greater than his grace, The storm cannot hide his bless-ed face; I am sat-is-fied to know That with Je-sus here be-low, I can con-quer ev-'ry foe.

By permission of Ballington Booth. Copyrighted.

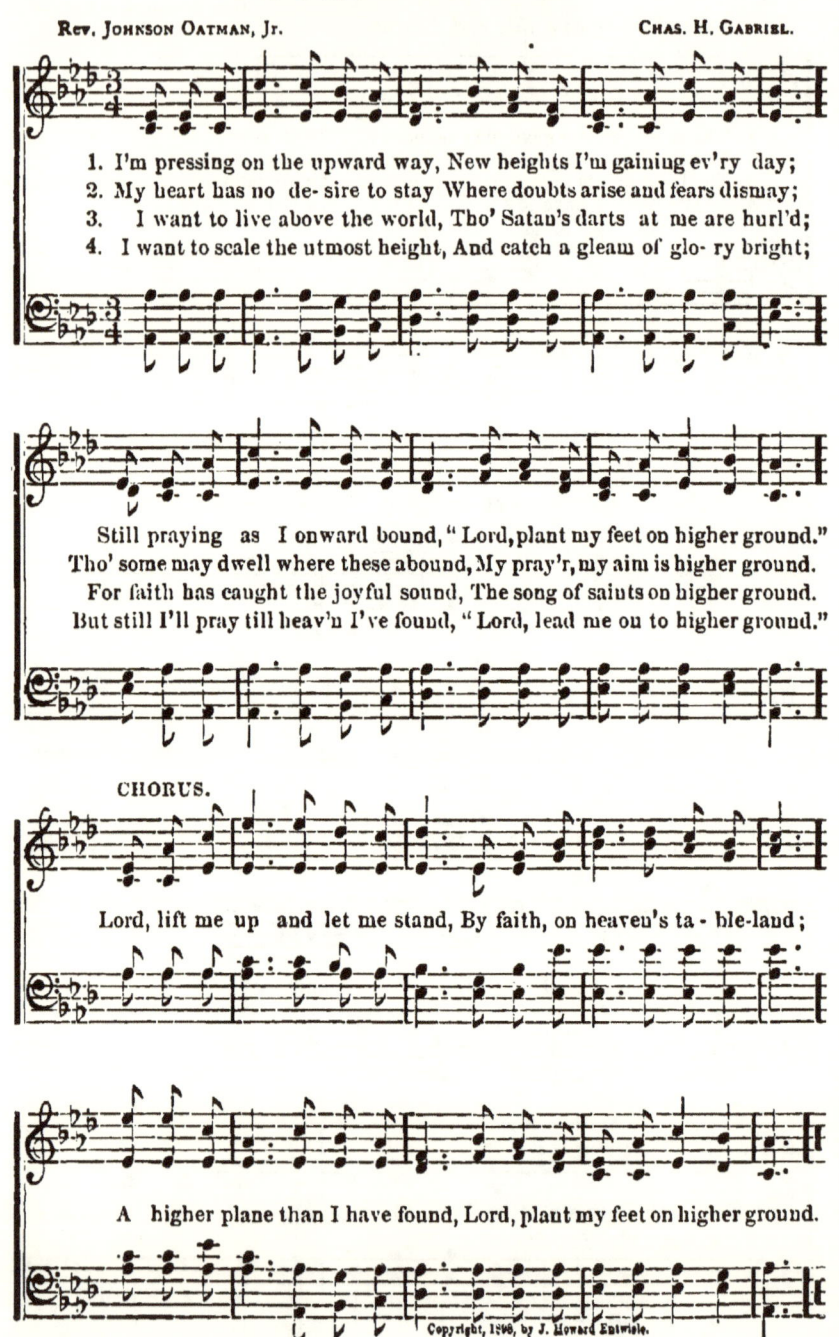

18. Happy All the Day.

Rev. Johnson Oatman, Jr. J. Howard Entwisle.

1. Once I was heavy la-den, Borne down with sin and woe, I cried out "who will help me, Ah, whither shall I go?" I heard a sweet voice an-swer, "I am the Life, the Way," And since I turned to Je-sus
2. No more my way is drear-y, My heart is full of spring, No time for dull re-pin-ing, For now I shout and sing; I'm glad I sought his fa-vor, I'm glad I learned to pray, For since I've been forgiv-en
3. My life is full of sunshine, My soul is full of love, I'm on my way to heav-en, That gold-en land a-bove; I'm glad I ev-er en-tered The straight and narrow way, For here I find such glo-ry,
4. Some day I'll reach the cit-y Where my fair mansion stands, And there en-joy for-ev-er "That house not made with hands;" But while my blessed Saviour, Is with me on the way, It seems so much like heaven,

CHORUS.

I'm happy all the day. I'm happy all the day, I'm happy all the way; Yes, since I found my Saviour I'm happy all the day.
hap-py all the day, hap-py all the way;

Copyright, 1898, by J. Howard Entwisle.

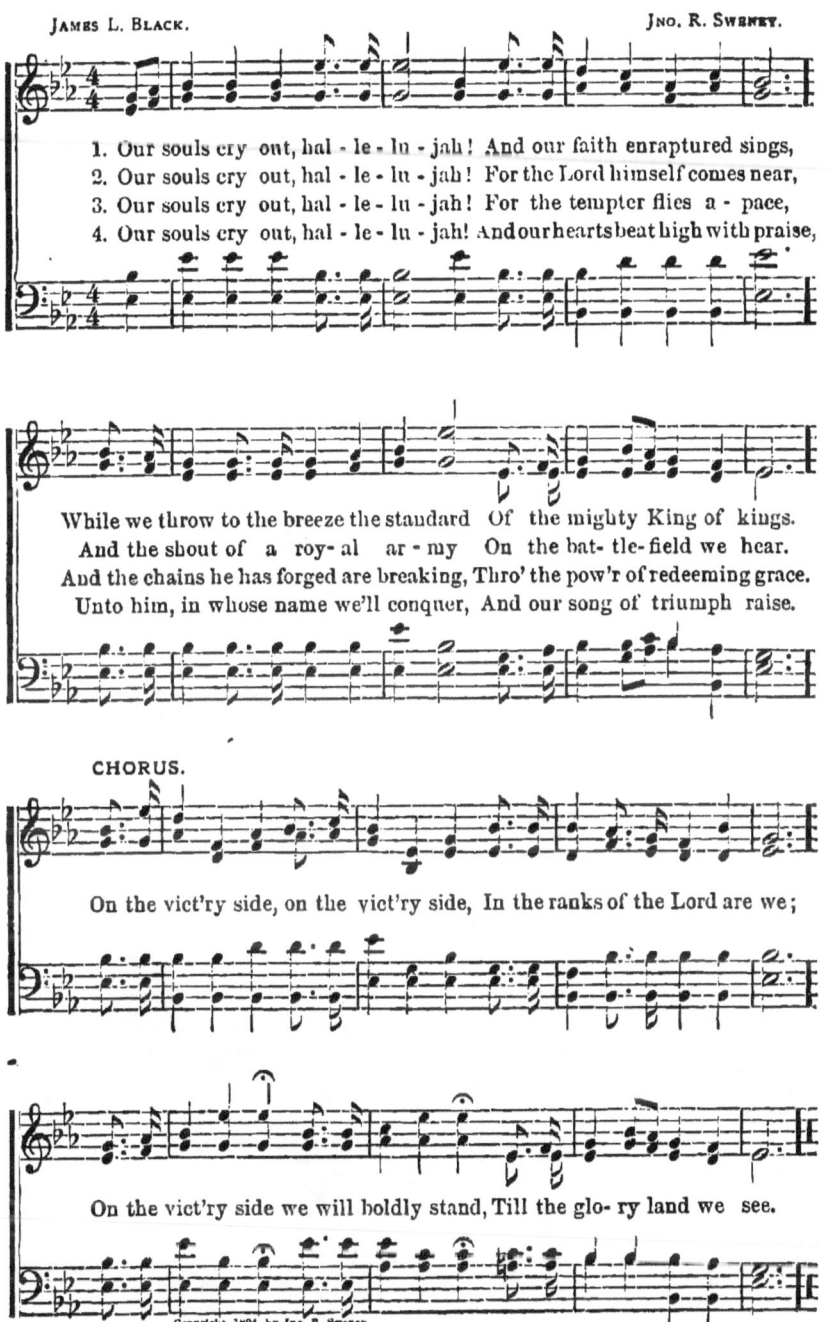

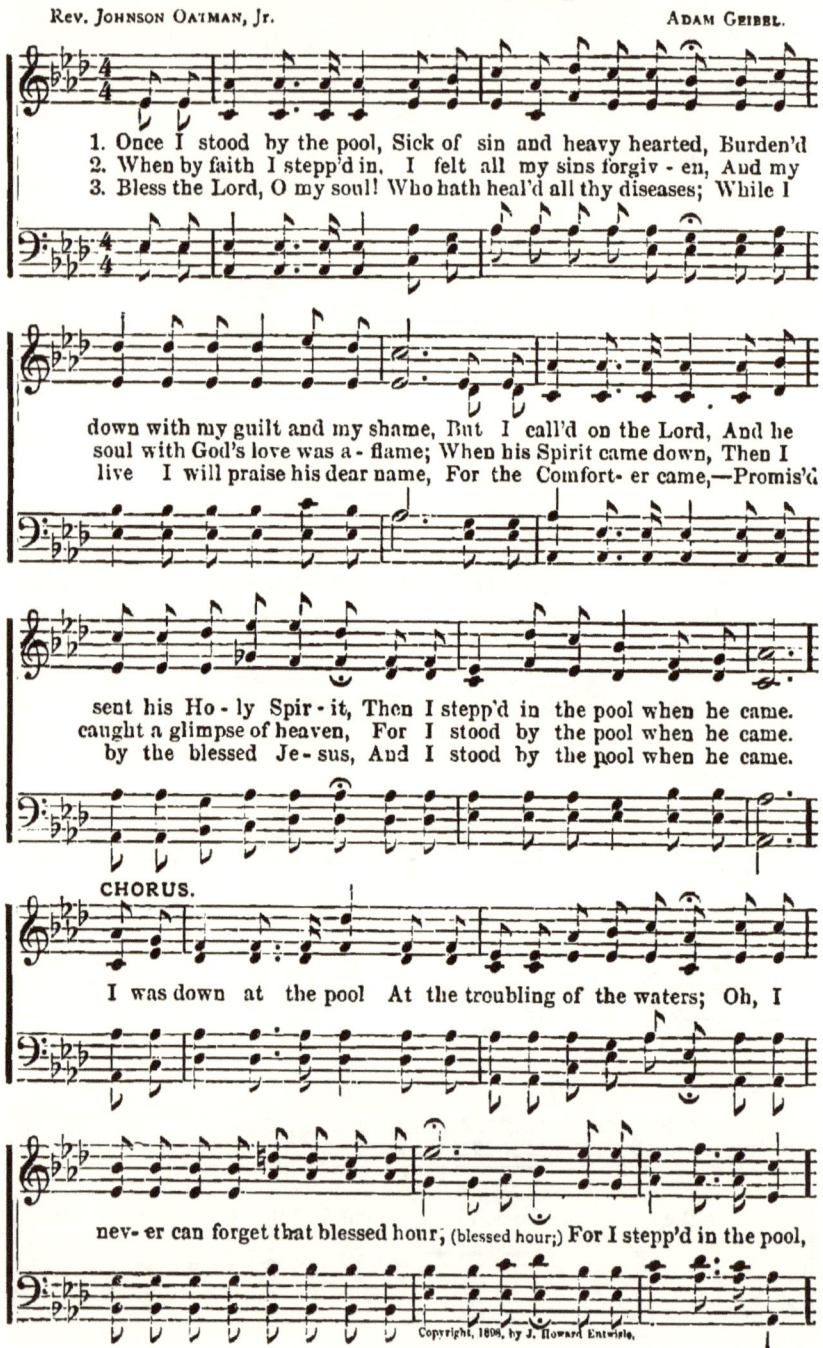

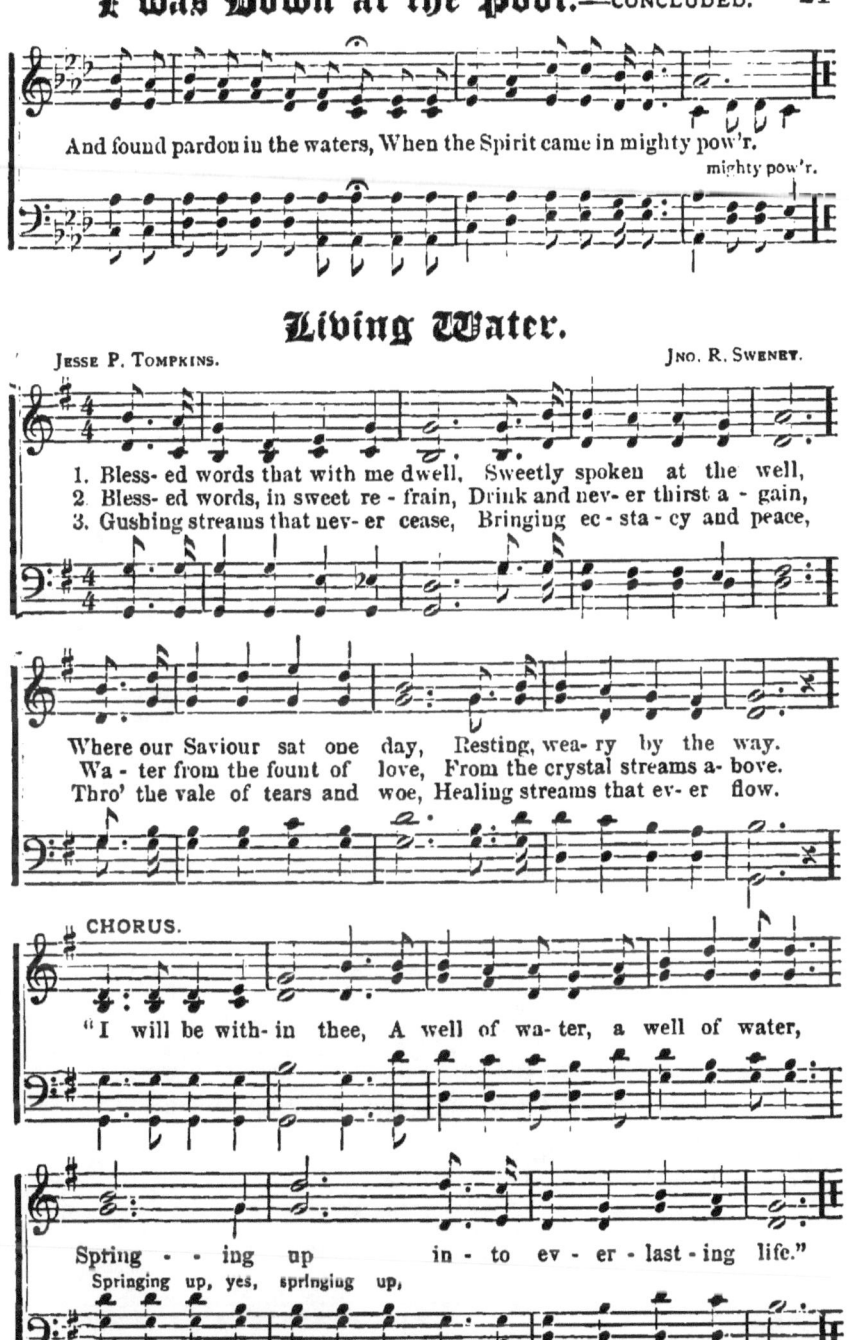

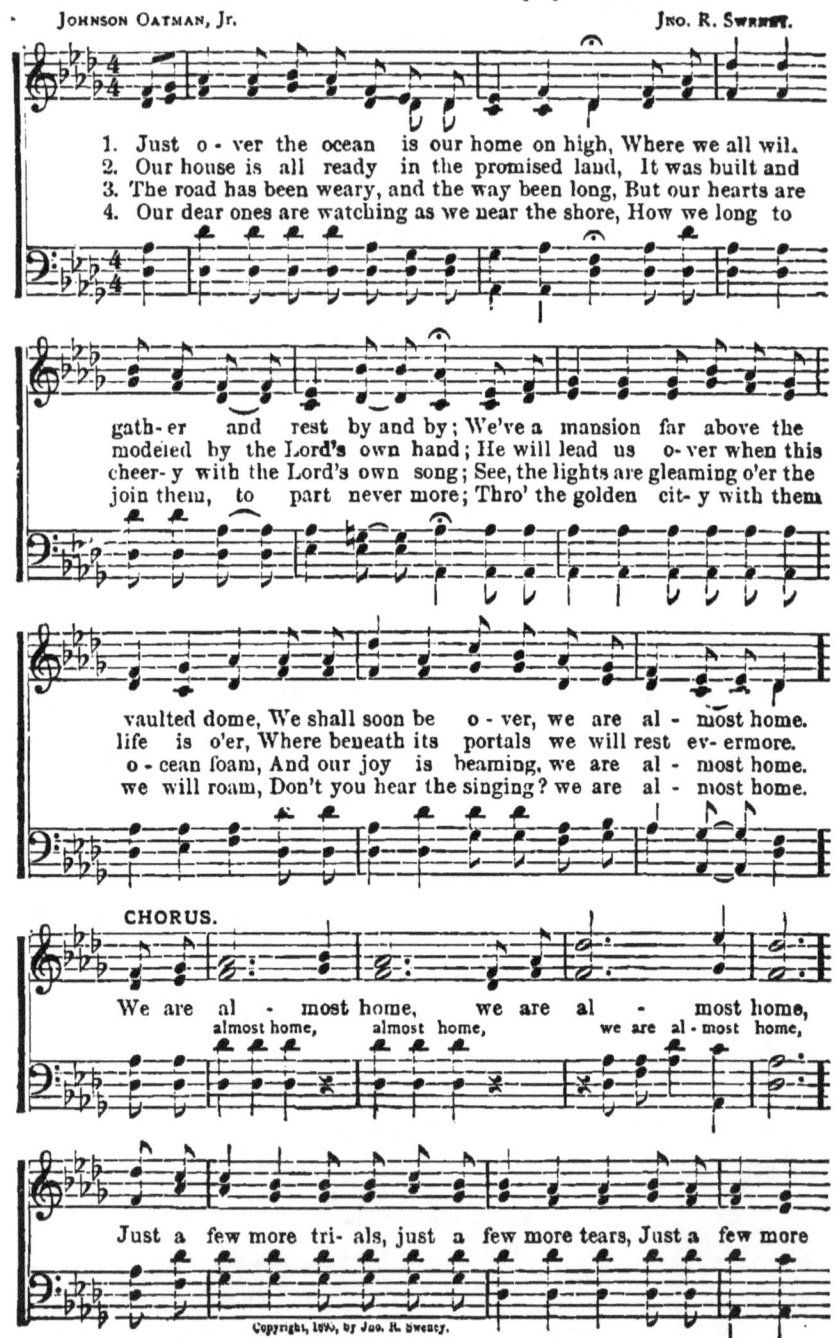

We are Almost Home.—CONCLUDED.

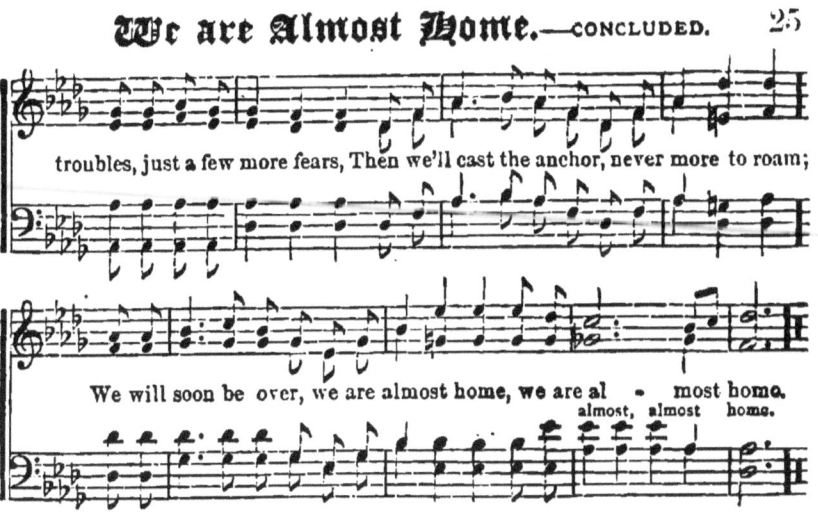

troubles, just a few more fears, Then we'll cast the anchor, never more to roam;
We will soon be over, we are almost home, we are al - most home.
almost, almost home.

The Golden Key.

"Prayer is the key to unlock the door, and the bolt to shut in the night"

JNO. R. SWENEY.

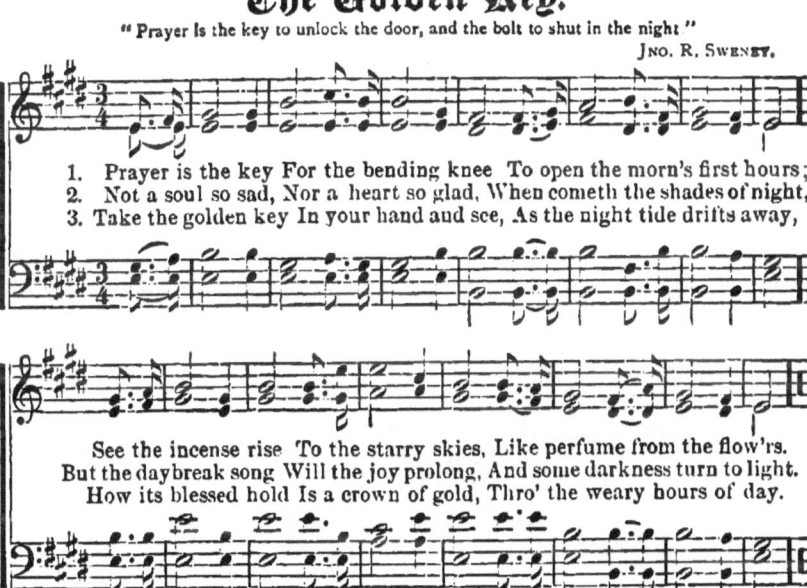

1. Prayer is the key For the bending knee To open the morn's first hours;
2. Not a soul so sad, Nor a heart so glad, When cometh the shades of night,
3. Take the golden key In your hand and see, As the night tide drifts away,

See the incense rise To the starry skies, Like perfume from the flow'rs.
But the daybreak song Will the joy prolong, And some darkness turn to light.
How its blessed hold Is a crown of gold, Thro' the weary hours of day.

Copyright, 1875, by John J. Hood.

4 When the shadows fall,
And the vesper call
Is sobbing its low refrain,
'Tis a garland sweet
To the toil-dent feet,
And an antidote for pain.

5 Soon the year's dark door
Shall be shut no more:
Life's tears shall be wiped away,
As the pearl gates swing,
And the gold harps ring,
And the sun unsheathes for aye.

Praise Hymns—D

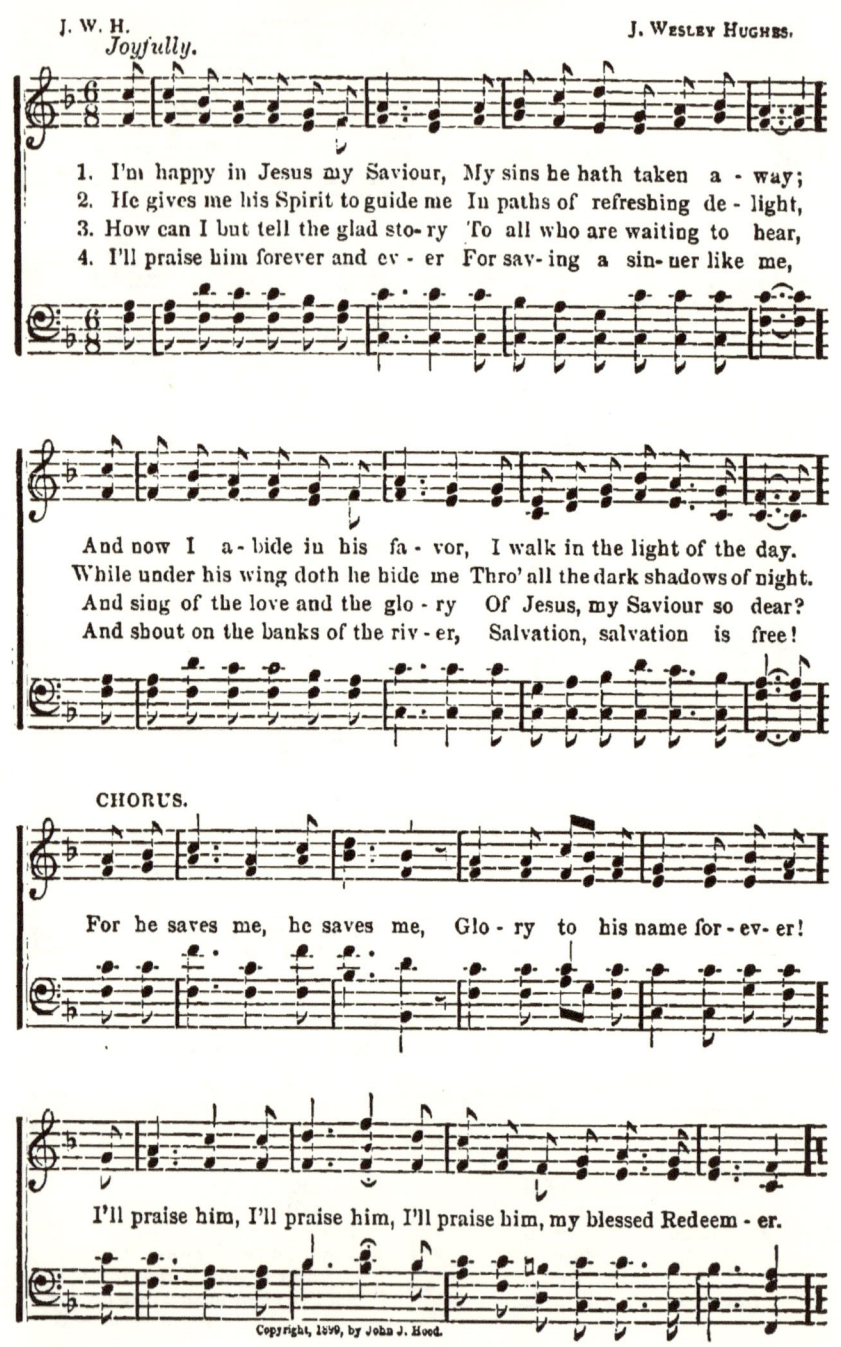

4 Tho' life's storms may sweep around
  In my soul I sing and shout, [me,
  For I know that every tempest
  Will but drive me farther out.

5 Farther out, till I have safely
  Reached that land across the foam,
  Farther out, till I have anchored
  In the soul's eternal home.

Nearer every Day.

Rev. Johnson Oatman, Jr. — Adam Geibel.

1. To my blessed Lord and Saviour, as he walks before me here, I am getting nearer, nearer ev-'ry day; And he says I shall be like him when be-fore him I ap-pear, And I'm getting nearer, nearer ev-'ry day.
2. To the pure and perfect stature of our great and living Head, I am getting nearer, nearer ev-'ry day; To the perfect will of Je-sus in the way that I am led, I am getting nearer, nearer ev-'ry day.
3. To the time when I shall gladly lay my cross and burdens down, I am getting nearer, nearer ev-'ry day; To the time when from my Saviour I'll re-ceive a robe and crown, I am getting nearer, nearer ev-'ry day.
4. To that blest e-ter-nal cit-y that lies just across the foam, I am getting nearer, nearer ev-'ry day; Oft-en thro' faith's open vis-ion I can see the spires of home, And I'm getting nearer, nearer ev-'ry day.

CHORUS.

Ev'ry day, praise the Lord, I'm getting nearer, And the way, praise the Lord, is getting clearer; From my Lord no more I'll roam,

Copyright, 1898, by J. Howard Entwisle.

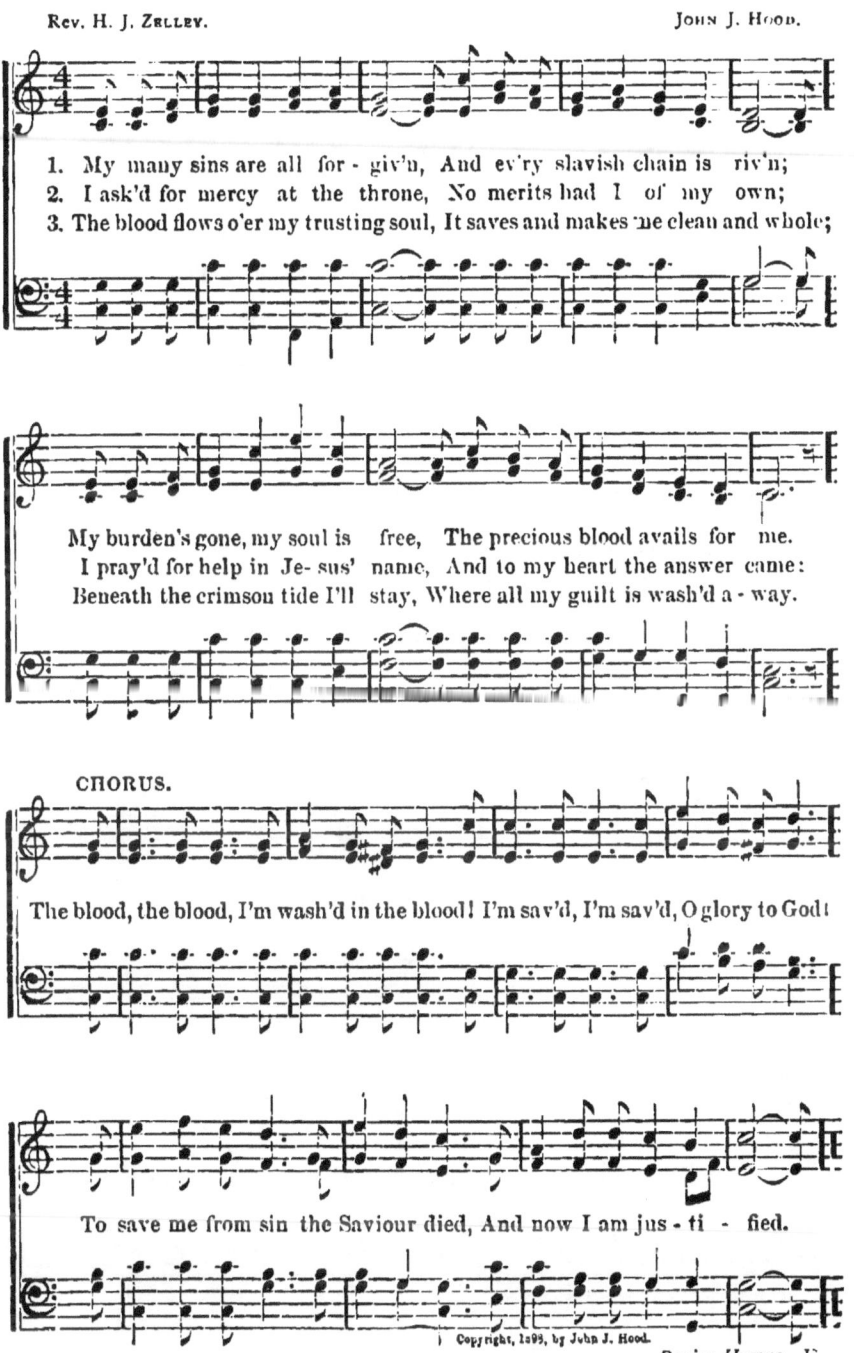

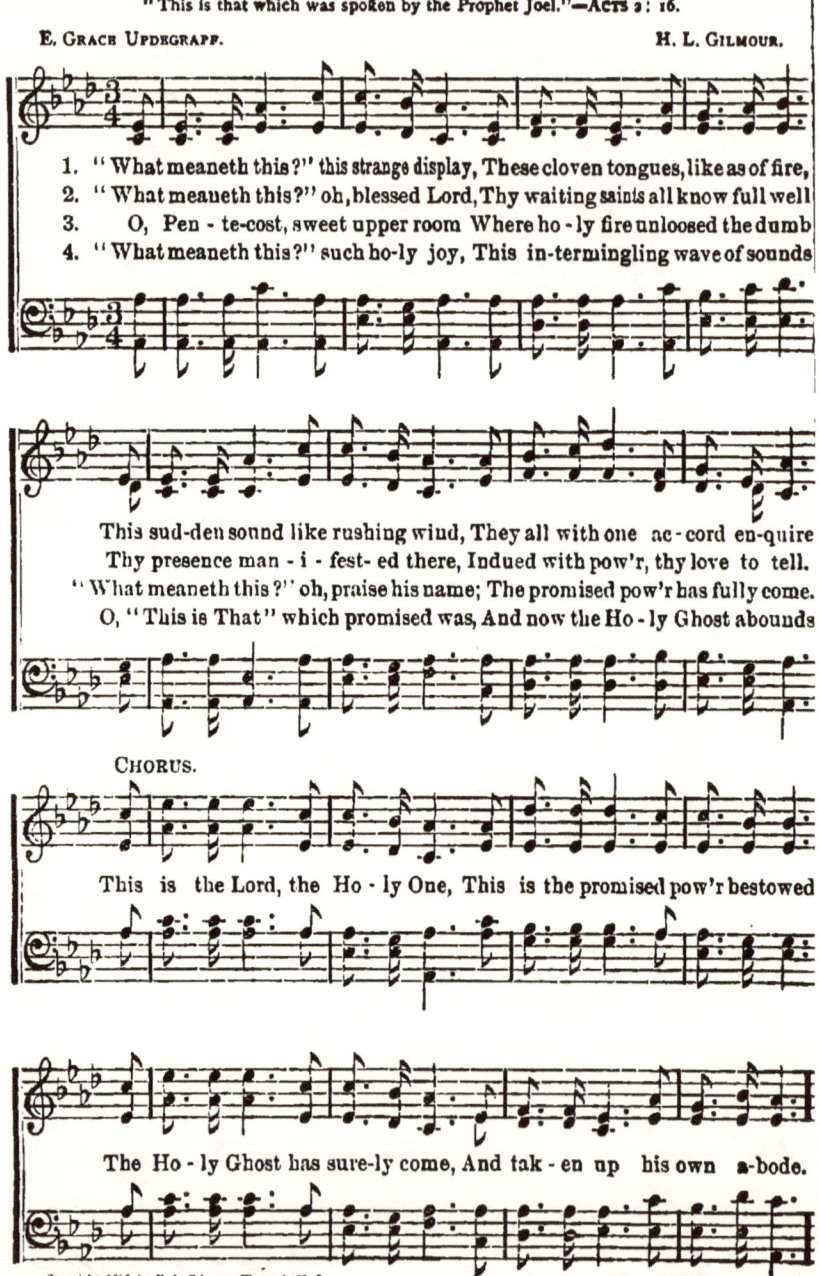

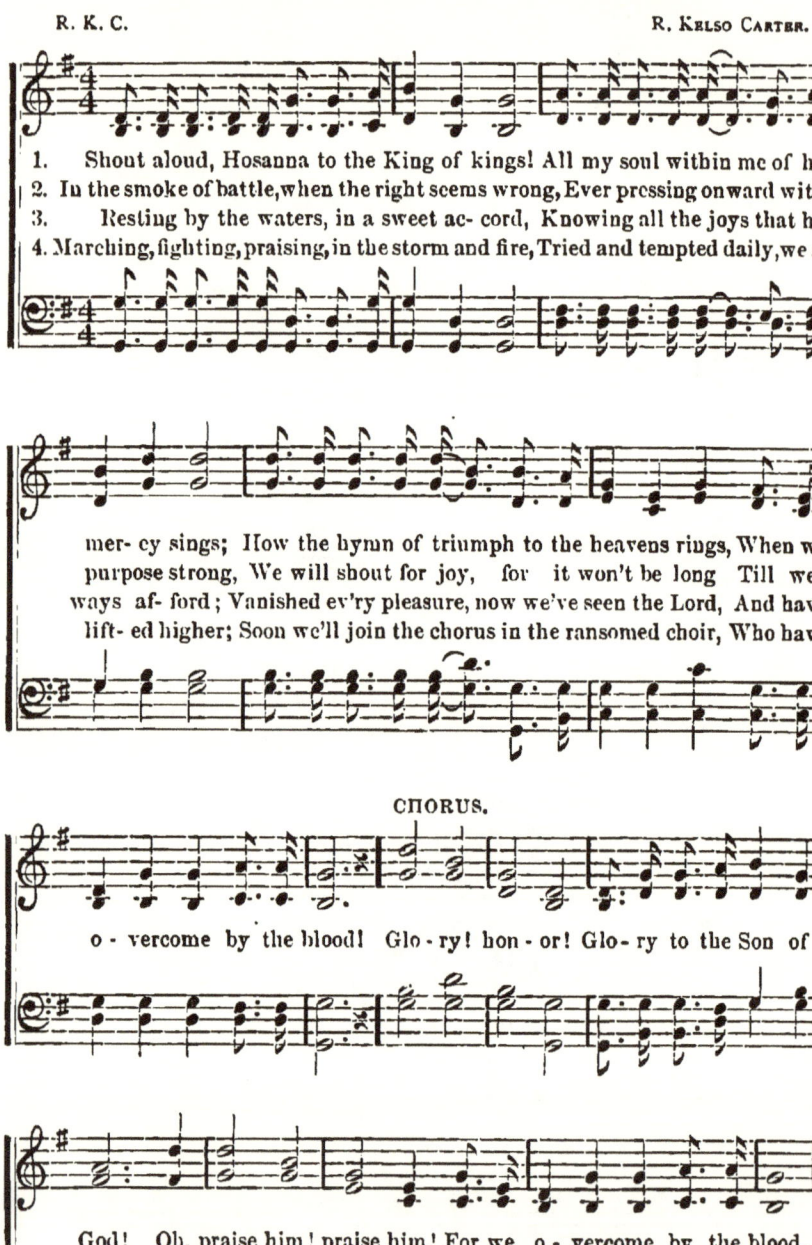

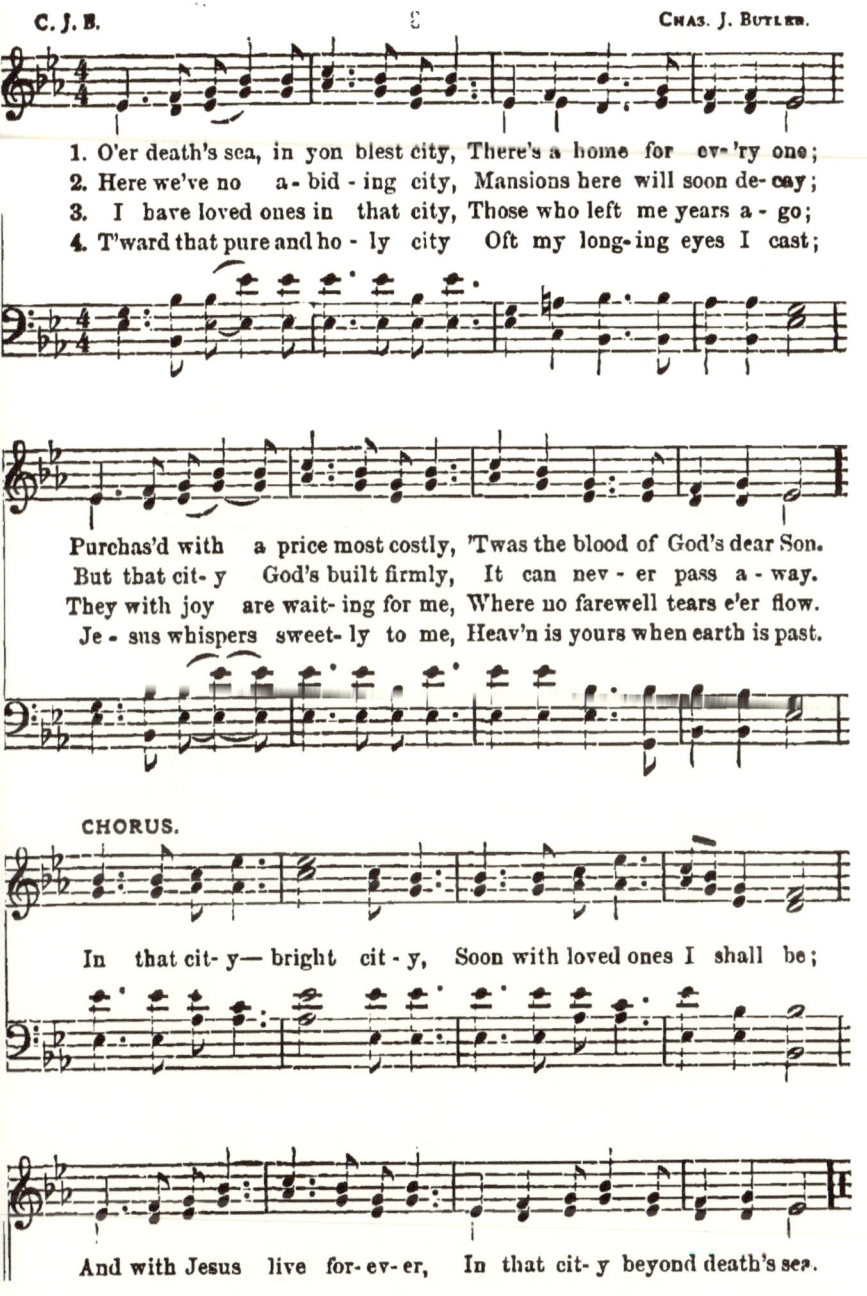

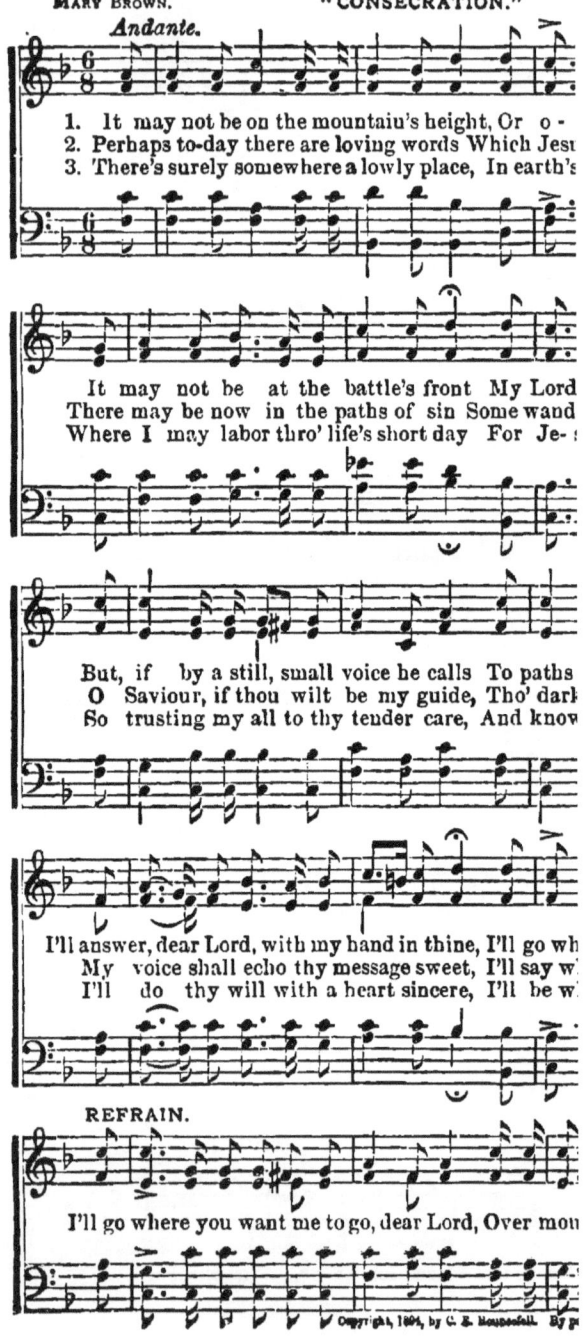

I'll Go where You, etc.—CONCLUDED. 47

y what you want me to say, dear Lord, I'll be what you want me to be.

Don't You Know He Cares?

jah, when he sat under the Juniper tree and prayed for the Lord to take his life, how often of trouble, sit under our Juniper tree of sorrow alone and cry out, " I am passing through nd ' Nobody Cares.'"

HNSON OATMAN, Jr.   J. HOWARD ENTWISLE.

'hen your spirit bows in sor-row   From the load it bears,   Go and
[ave your feet become entan-gled   In the tempter's snares? There is
[ave you been by grief o'ertak-en,   Stricken un-awares?   Yet you
Is your body fill'd with anguish,   With the pain it bears? Think of

Fine. CHORUS.

. your heart to Jesus,—Don't you know he cares? Yes, there is One who
who died to save you, Don't you know he cares?
ll not be for-sak-en, Don't you know he cares?
the Saviour suffered—Don't you know he cares?

D.S.—Don't you know he cares?

D.S.

s your burdens, Ev'ry sorrow shares; Go and tell it all to Je-sus,—

Copyright, 1897, by John J. Hood.

' friends and loss of fortune—
a dark look wears;
: Saviour still is with you,
t you know he cares?

6 So amid life's cares and struggles,
Blending songs with prayers—
Always put your trust in Jesus,
Don't you know he cares?

Waiting at the Mercy Seat.

Mrs. C. H. M. Mrs. C. H. Morris.

1. Father, thou art willing to bestow The Spirit's pow'r upon thy children;
2. Search me, Lord, and know this heart of mine, Have I surrender'd to thee fully?
3. As the branches of the Living Vine, Are we, thy children, now abiding?

And we cannot, cannot let thee go Until the precious boon is giv-en.
Is my will completely lost in thine, The Spirit's dwelling place made holy?
May we claim the promis'd pow'r divine To all who come in faith confiding.

REFRAIN.

Waiting at the mer-cy seat, O Father, We are waiting at the mer-cy

seat; For the Spirit's pow'r and blessing, Waiting at the mercy seat.

Copyright, 1898, by John J. Hood.

4 Bid us not go hence nor leave thy throne,
   Until thy Spirit thou'rt bestowing;
   Till in us thy perfect will be done,
   And all the fullness we are knowing.

5 Hush'd the raging tempest in my soul,
   As Christ to peace the storm is stilling;
   Waves of comfort now above me roll,
   As he with love my soul is filling.

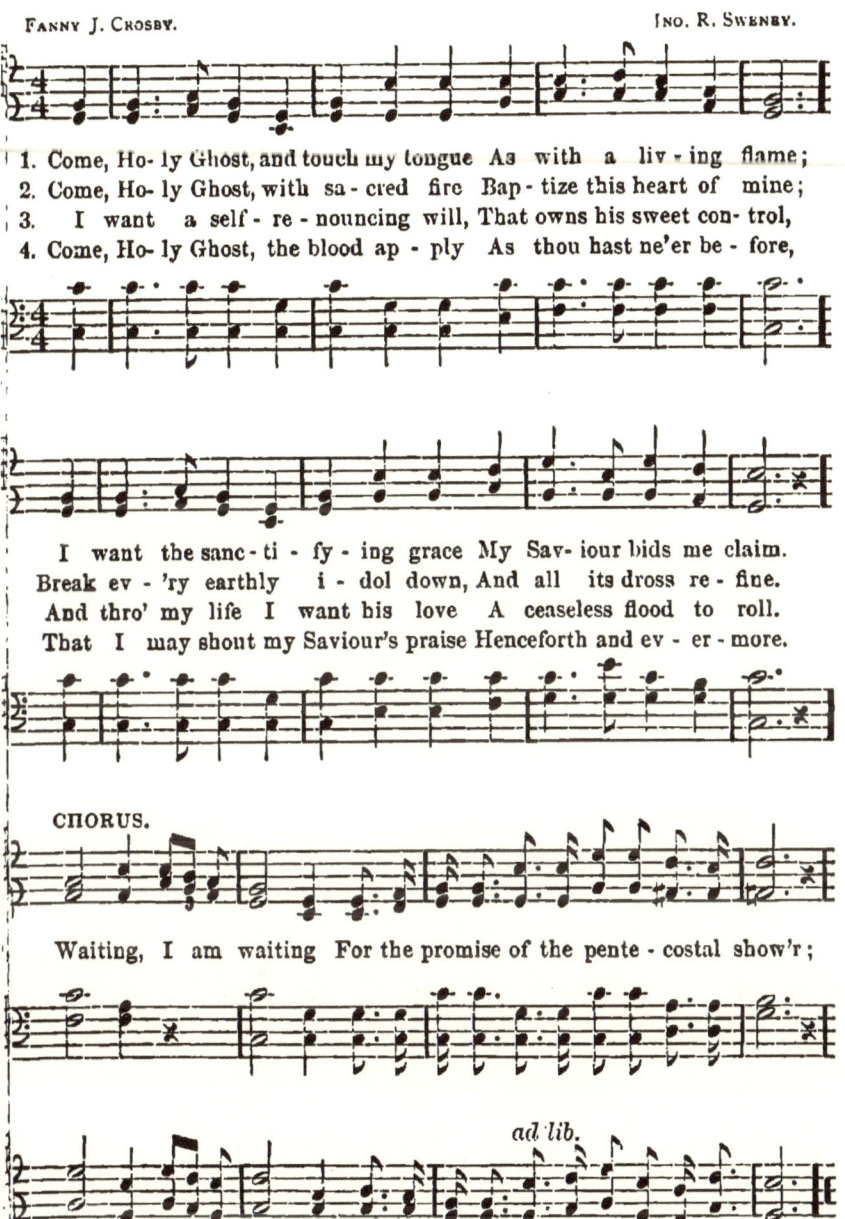

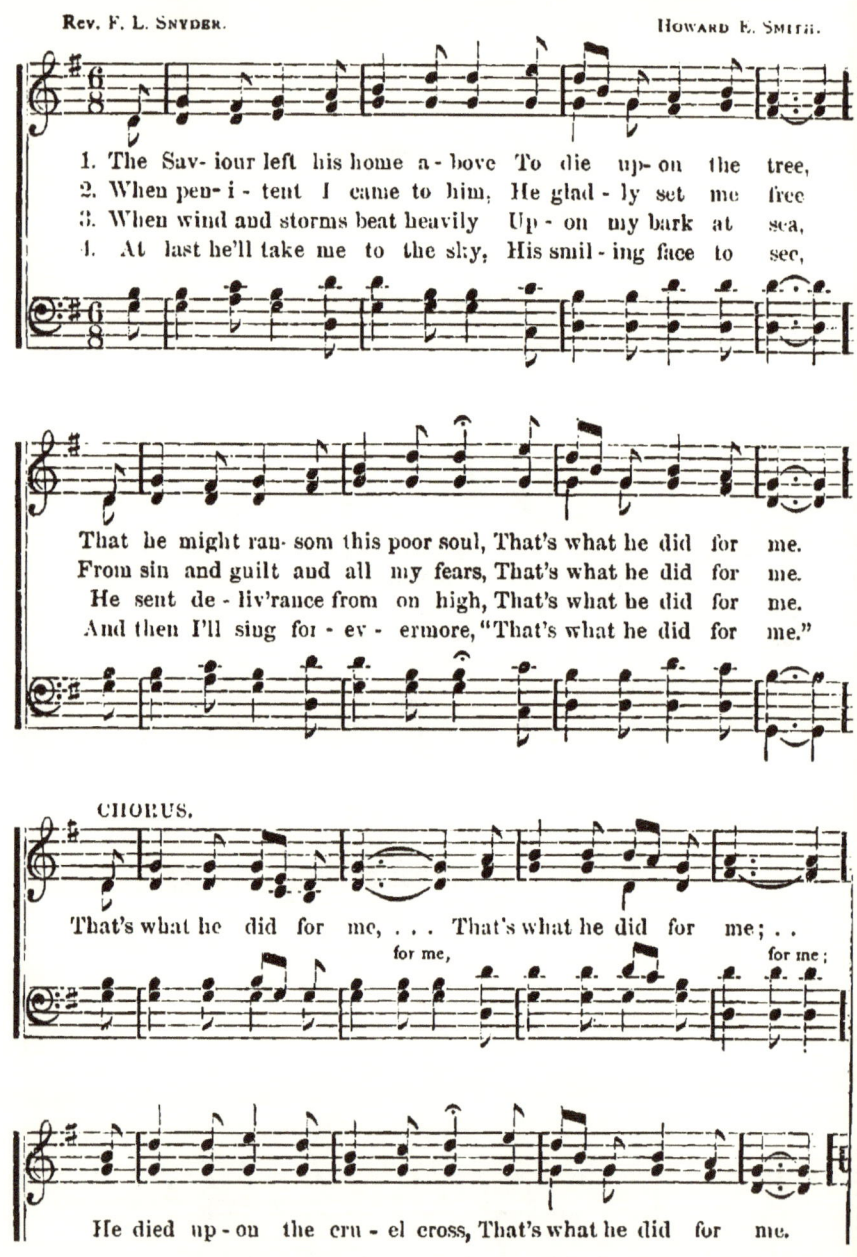

53 How Firm a Foundation.
M. E. H. 679.

How firm a foundation, ye saints
 of the Lord,
Is laid for your faith in his excel-
 lent word!
What more can he say, than to you
 he hath said,
To you, who for refuge to Jesus
 have fled?

2 "Fear not, I am with thee, O be
  not dismayed
 For I am thy God, I will still give
  thee aid;
 I'll strengthen thee, help thee, and
  cause thee to stand,
 Upheld by my gracious, omnipotent
  hand.

3 "When thro' the deep waters I call
  thee to go,
 The rivers of sorrow shall not over-
  flow;
 For I will be with thee thy trials
  to bless,
 And sanctify to thee thy deepest
  distress.

4 "When through fiery trials thy
  pathway shall lie,
 My grace, all-sufficient, shall be thy
  supply,
 The flame shall not hurt thee; I
  only design
 Thy dross to consume, and thy gold
  to refine.

5 "E'en down to old age all my peo-
  ple shall prove
 My sovereign, eternal, unchangeable love;
 And when hoary hairs shall their
  temples adorn
 Like lambs they shall still in my
  bosom be borne.

64 Step Out on the Promise.
Music No. 191 in "Precious Hymns."

O MOURNER in Zion, how blessed
  art thou,
For Jesus is waiting to comfort
  thee now,
Fear not to rely on the word of
  thy God;
Step out on the promise,—get under
  the blood.

2 O ye that are hungry and thirsty,
   rejoice!
 For ye shall be filled; do you hear
  that sweet voice
 Inviting you now to the banquet of
  God?
 Step out on the promise,—get under
  the blood.

3 Who sighs for a heart from iniqui-
  ty free?
 O poor troubled soul! there's a
  promise for thee.
 There's rest, weary one, in the
  bosom of God;
 Step out on the promise,—get under
  the blood.

4 Step out on the promise, and Christ
  you shall win,
 "The blood of his Son cleanseth us
  from all sin,"
 It cleanseth me now, hallelujah to
  God!
 I rest on the promise,—I'm under
  the blood.

5 The promise don't save, tho' the
  promise is true;
 'Tis the blood we get under that
  cleanseth us through,
 It cleanseth me now, hallelujah to
  God!
 I rest on the promise,—I'm under
  the blood.

55 I'm a Holiness Christian.
Tune, "Jesus Listening All the Day."

I'M a Holiness Christian,
 From the wilderness I came,
I'm saved and washed in Jesus' blood,
 Hallelujah to His name.

CHO.—I'm a Holiness Christian,
  I'm so happy all the time,
 I sing, I shout, I leap for joy,
  And oh, it is sublime.

I came down to Jordan's river,
 When the current was so strong,
I plunged right in and came straight
  through
 With a hallelujah song.

I came then to old Jericho,
 Oh! the walls were very high,
I gave a shout, and down they came,
 And the Canaanites did fly.

I am dwelling now in Beulah,
 Where the sun shines all the time;
I live on figs and grapes and corn,
 In a hallelujah clime,

FAMILIAR HYMNS.

56. Treasures of Heaven.
Tune in "Songs of Redeeming Love," p. 49.

THERE'S a crown in heaven for the striving soul,
Which the blessed Jesus himself will place
On the head of each who shall faithful prove,
Even unto death, in the heavenly race.

CHO.—Oh, may that crown in heaven be mine.
And I among the angels shine;
Be thou, O Lord! my daily guide,
Let me ever in thy love abide.

2 There's a joy in heaven for the mourning soul,
Though the tears may fall all the earthly night;
Yet the clouds of sadness will break away,
And rejoicing come with the morning light.

CHO.—Oh, may that joy, etc.

3 There's a home in heaven for the faithful soul,
In the many mansions prepared above,
Where the glorified shall forever sing,
Of a Saviour's free and unbounded love.

CHO.—Oh, may that home, etc.

T. C. O'KANE.

57. Higher Than I.

OH, sometimes the shadows are deep,
And rough seems the path to the goal,
And sorrows, how often they sweep,
Like tempests, down over the soul.

CHO.—||: Oh, then to the Rock let me fly,
To the Rock that is higher than I. :||

2 Oh, sometimes, how long seems the day,
And sometimes how weary my feet;
But toiling in life's dusty way,
The Rock's blessed shadow how sweet!

3 Oh, near to the Rock let me keep,
Or blessings or sorrows prevail;
Or climbing the mountain-way steep,
Or walking the shadowy vale.

E. JOHNSON.

58. The Child of a King.
Music No. 87, "Hymn Songs."

MY Father is rich in houses an lands,
He holdeth the wealth of the worl in his hands!
Of rubies and diamonds, of silve and gold,
His coffers are full, he has riche untold.

CHO.—I'm the child of a King, th child of a King,
With Jesus my Saviour, I'm th child of a King.

2 My Father's own Son, the "Saviou of men!"
Once wandered o'er earth as th poorest of them;
But now he is reigning, forever o high,
And will give me a home in th sweet by and by!

3 I once was an out-cast stranger o earth,
A sinner by choice, an alien b birth!
But I've been adopted, my name written down;
An heir to a mansion, a robe, and crown.

4 A tent or a cottage, why should care?
They're building a palace for m over there!
Though exiled from home, yet sti I may sing:
All glory to God, I'm the child a King.

HATTIE E. BUEL

59. The Land that has no Storm.

SINNER, whither art thou going,
Heedless of the clouds that form
Satan tries his best to keep you
From the land that has no storn

CHO.—I'm going, yes, I'm going
To the land that has no storn

2 Sinner, wake, and look around the
Light is breaking on the morn;
See the millions, hear them singin
In the land that has no storm.

3 Sinner, earth is full of sorrow.
Full of trial and of scorn;
Won't you come, and be with Jesu
In the land that hath no storm?

60. The Lion of Judah.

From "The Quiver." Tune, No. 142.

'TWAS Jesus, my Saviour, who died on the tree,
To open a fountain for sinners like me;
His blood is the fountain that pardon bestows,
And cleanses the foulest wherever it flows.

CHO.—For the Lion of Judah shall break every chain,
And give us the victory again and again.

2 And when I was willing with all things to part,
He gave me my bounty, his love in my heart;
So now I am joined with the conquering band,
Who are marching to glory at Jesus' command.

3 And when the last trumpet of judgment shall sound,
And wake all the nations that sleep in the ground,
Then, when heav'n and earth shall be melting away,
I'll sing of the blood of the cross in that day.

61. Are You Ready?

Music, No. 26 in "Precious Hymns."

SHOULD the summons, quickly flying,
On the slumb'ring nations fall,—
"Lo! the heavenly Bridegroom cometh,"
Would the sound your soul appal?
Are you ready? are you ready?
Should you hear the midnight call?

2 What if now the startling mandate
Should the sleeping virgins hear,—
Are your lamps all trimmed and burning,
Should the Bridegroom now appear?
Are you ready? are you ready?
Now to see your Lord appear?

3 Is there oil in all your vessels?
Are your garments pure and white?
Are they washed in the cleansing fountain,—
Fit to stand in Jesus' sight?
Are you ready? are you ready?
Are your lamps all clear and bright?

62. Come, Ye Sinners.

COME, ye sinners, poor and needy,
Weak and wounded, sick and sore;
Jesus ready stands to save you,
Full of pity, love and power.

CHO.—Don't you hear the angels singing?
Hallelujah, hallelujah;
Don't you hear the angels singing?
Glory be to God on high!

2 Now, ye needy, come and welcome;
God's free bounty glorify;
True belief and true repentance,
Every grace that brings you nigh.

3 Let not conscience make you linger,
Nor of fitness fondly dream;
All the fitness he requireth
Is to feel the need of him.

4 Come, ye weary, heavy-laden,
Bruised and mangled by the fall;
If you tarry till you're better,
You will never come at all.

63. A Sinner Like Me.

Music No. 111 in "Precious Hymns."

I WAS once far away from the Saviour,
And as vile as a sinner could be,
I wondered if Christ, the Redeemer,
Could save a poor sinner like me.

2 I wandered on in the darkness,
Not a ray of light could I see,
And the thought filled my heart with sadness,
There's no hope for a sinner like me.

3 And then, in that dark, lonely hour,
A voice sweetly whispered to me,
Saying, Christ, the Redeemer, hath power
To save a poor sinner like me.

4 I listened, and lo! 'twas the Saviour
That was speaking so kindly to me;
I cried, I'm the chief of sinners,
Thou canst save a poor sinner like me.

5 I then fully trusted in Jesus,
And oh, what a joy came to me;
My heart was filled with his praises
For saving a sinner like me.

6 And when life's journey is over,
And I the dear Saviour shall see,
I'll praise him forever and ever,
For saving a sinner like me.

CHAS. J. BUTLER.

FAMILIAR HYMNS.

64   **Wondrous Love.**
Tune in "Goodly Pearls," p. 59.

God loved the world of sinners lost,
   And ruined by the fall;
Salvation full, at highest cost,
   He offers free to all.

Cho.—Oh, 'twas love, 'twas wondrous love!
   The love of God to me;
It brought my Saviour from above,
   To die on Calvary.

2 E'n now by faith I claim him mine,
   The risen Son of God;
Redemption by his death I find,
   And cleansing through his blood.

3 Love brings the glorious fulness in,
   And to his saints makes known
The blessed rest from inbred sin,
   Through faith in Christ alone.

65   **Jesus Saves Me.**

Precious Saviour, thou hast saved me;
   Thine and only thine I am;
Oh, the cleansing blood has reached me,
   Glory, glory to the Lamb!

Cho.—Glory, glory, Jesus saves me,
   Glory, glory to the Lamb!
Oh, the cleansing blood has reached me,
   Glory, glory, to the Lamb!

2 Long my yearning heart was trying
   To enjoy this perfect rest;
But I gave all trying over;
   Simply trusting, I was blest.

3 Trusting, trusting every moment;
   Feeling now the blood applied;
Lying at the cleansing fountain;
   Dwelling in my Saviour's side.

4 Consecrated to thy service,
   I will live and die to thee;
I will witness to thy glory
   Of salvation full and free.
                     Louise M. Rouse.

66   **Yes, I Will Rejoice.**
From "Songs of Redeeming Love."
Tune, p. 30.

Though troubles assail, and dangers affright,
Though friends should all fail, and foes all unite,
Yet one thing secures us, whatever betide,
The promise assures us "The Lord will provide."

Cho.—||:Yes, I will rejoice, rejoice the Lord,:||
Will joy in the God of my salvati(on)

2 The birds, without barn or st(ore) house, are fed,
From them let us learn to trust our bread;
His saints what is fitting shall n(ot) be denied,
So long as 'tis written, "The L(ord) will provide."

3 When Satan appears to stop up (the) path,
And fills us with fears, we triu(mph) by faith;
He cannot take from us, though he has tried,
The heart-cheering promise, "(The) Lord will provide."

4 He tells us we're weak, our hop(es) in vain;
The good that we seek we n(e'er) shall obtain;
But when such suggestions graces have tried,
This answers all questions, "(The) Lord will provide."

67   **Lights Along the Shore.**

I'm a pilgrim and a stranger pass(ing) over,
The road may be rough, but clear,
And a starry crown awaits me (at) the river,
And Jesus bids me welcome th(ere).

Cho.—There are lights along (the) shore that never grow dim,
That never, never grow dim;
These souls are all aflame
With the love of Jesus' name,
They guide us, yes, they guide unto him.

2 Sometimes I meet with trials on (my) journey,
Temptation and sorrow by (the) way;
But Jesus speaks, and says, "(I'm) ever near thee,
To guide to realms of end(less) day."

3 Friends of Jesus! may your li(ght) be trimmed and burning,
And shining along the way (of) love;
Soon you'll gain the heights (of) glory, and be singing
The happy song of saints abo(ve).
                     Rev. J. H. Stock(ton)

70. Go, Seek Until Ye Find.

Music No. 237 in "The Temple Trio."

ALAS! alas! a wayward sheep
  Had wandered from the fold,
Far o'er the mountains rough and
    steep,
  Where howling tempests rolled;
The Shepherd, with a burdened
    mind,
  Went forth the missing one to find,
The missing one, far, far away,
  The missing one to find.

CHO.—Go, seek until ye find,
  Go, seek until ye find;
The missing one must not be lost—
  Go, seek until ye find.

2 He sought, with many a footstep
    sore,
  From early morn till night;
Through rocky wastes, where tor-
    rents roar,—
  All pathways but the right;
Then cried, with sad and burdened
    mind,
  The missing I have failed to find,
The missing one, far, far away,
  Alas! I've failed to find.

71. Coming By and By.

Tune in "The Wells of Salvation," p. 168.

A BETTER day is coming,
  A morning bright and fair;
If we live right, both day and night,
  We'll have a home up there;
God's only Son will listen
  To every creature's sigh,
Have mercy here and everywhere,
  And take us by and by.

CHO.—Coming by and by, coming by
    and by,
  A better day is coming, the time is
    drawing nigh,
Coming by and by, coming by and
    by,
  Our days are few, we'll soon pass
    through,
'Tis coming by and by.

2 A better day is coming,
  We cannot say how long,
'Twill glory be when we shall see
  The host around the throne,
Then free from want and sorrow,
  Our tears will all be dry,
We'll sing and shine, 'mid light
    divine,
  In glory by and by.

FAMILIAR HYMNS.

72 All Hail the Power.

ALL hail the power of Jesus' name!
Let angels prostrate fall;
Bring forth the royal diadem,
And crown him Lord of all.

2 Sinners, whose love can ne'er forget
The wormwood and the gall,
Go, spread your trophies at his feet,
And crown him Lord of all.

3 Let every kindred, every tribe,
On this terrestrial ball,
To him all majesty ascribe,
And crown him Lord of all.

4 O that with yonder sacred throng
We at his feet may fall!
We'll join the everlasting song,
And crown him Lord of all.

73 Memories of Galilee.

Music No. 75 in "The Quartet."

EACH cooing dove and sighing bough,
That makes the eve so blest to me,
Has something far diviner now,
It bears me back to Galilee.

CHO.—O Galilee! sweet Galilee!
Where Jesus loved so much to be;
O Galilee! blue Galilee!
Come, sing thy song again to me!

2 Each flowery glen and mossy dell,
Where happy birds in song agree,
Through sunny morn the praises tell
Of sights and sounds in Galilee.

3 And when I read the thrilling lore
Of him who walked upon the sea,
I long, oh, how I long once more
To follow him in Galilee.

74 Who is He?

WHO is he in yonder stall,
At whose feet the shepherds fall?

CHO.—'Tis the Lord, oh, wondrous story,
'Tis the Lord, the King of glory,
At whose feet the shepherds fall,
Crown him, crown him Lord of all.

2 Who is he that stands and weeps
At the grave where Lazarus sleeps?

3 Who is he that on the cross
Bled for me and bled for all?

4 Who is he that from the grave
Comes to heal, and help, and save?

75 Where is your Soul?

Tune, "Where is My Wandering Boy To-night?"

WHERE is your soul, poor sinner, now,
Your soul for which Jesus died,
Your soul that is all with guilt defiled,
Your soul that has God defied.

CHO.—||: Oh, come to the Saviour now! :||
With outstretched hands,
See the Saviour, he stands;
Oh, come to the Saviour now.

2 Come to the Saviour while it is day,
The night it comes on apace,
To-day you may come; oh, cesus' just now,
For now is the day of grace.

3 Come to the Saviour, the blood is shed;
He finished the work for thee,
Come now, and just cast yourself on him,
Who died on the cursed tree.

4 Where are you wandering to, poor soul?
To darkness and black despair,
Where sinners forever dwell,
Be sure there's no mercy there.

76 Do you Triumph?

Do you triumph, oh my brother,
Over all this world of sin?
In each storm of tribulation
Does your Jesus reign within?

CHO.—I am reigning, sweetly reigning,
Far above this world of strife;
In my blessed, loving Saviour,
I am reigning in this life.

2 One we hail as King Immortal,
He did earth and hell subdue;
And bequeathing us his glory,
We are kings anointed too.

3 Shall we, then, by sin be humbled,
Must we yield to any foe?
No, by heaven's "gift" we're reigning
Over all this world below.

4 Oh, what grace and high promotion
That in Jesus I should be
Raised from sin to royal honor,
Even reigning, Lord, with thee.

5 All this life is blissful sunshine,
Earth is subject at our feet;
Heaven pours its richest blessing
Round our throne of love complete.

77. Take Me as I Am.
Music No. 75 in "Precious Hymns."

Just as I am, without one plea,
But that thy blood was shed for me,
And that thou bid'st me come to thee,
O Lamb of God, I come.

Cho.—Take me as I am, take me as I am,
Oh, bring thy free salvation nigh,
And take me as I am.

Just as I am, and waiting not
To rid my soul of one dark blot,
To thee, whose blood can cleanse each spot,
O Lamb of God, I come.

Just as I am, though tossed about
With many a conflict, many a doubt,
Fightings within, and fears without,
O Lamb of God, I come.

Just as I am thou wilt receive,
Wilt welcome, pardon, cleanse, relieve:
Because thy promise I believe,
O Lamb of God, I come.

78. Is My Name Written There?
Music No. 18 in "Precious Hymns."

Lord, I care not for riches,
Neither silver nor gold;
I would make sure of heaven,
I would enter the fold:
In the book of thy kingdom,
With its pages so fair,
Tell me, Jesus, my Saviour,
Is my name written there?

Cho.—Is my name written there,
On the page white and fair?
In the book of thy kingdom,
Is my name written there?

Lord, my sins they are many,
Like the sands of the sea;
But thy blood, O my Saviour,
Is sufficient for me;
For thy promise is written
In bright letters that glow,
"Though your sins be as scarlet,
I will make them like snow."

Oh! that beautiful city,
With its mansions of light,
With its glorified beings,
In pure garments of white;
Where no evil thing cometh
To despoil what is fair,
Where the angels are watching,—
Is my name written there?
M. A. K.

79. Glory! Glory!
Tune, "Around the Throne of God."

How pleasant thus to sing and praise,
In fellowship of love;
Then let us walk in wisdom's ways,
And reign with him above.

Cho.—Singing glory! glory!
Glory be to God on High!

2 How sweet 'twill be when we are there,
Away from grief and pain
Where all is peace, and joy, and love,
To never part again.

3 How pleasant 'tis to walk the ways
The truth and life proclaim;
O bear the sound these voices raise,—
Salvation through his name!

4 O haste away, the time is nigh,
Have all your sins forgiven,
The angel's coming from the sky
To take us home to heav'n.

80. My Home is There.

Above the waves of earthly strife,
Above the ills and cares of life,
Where all is peaceful, bright and fair,
My home is there, my home is there.

Cho.—My beautiful home, my beautiful home
In the land where the glorified ever shall roam,
Where angels bright wear crowns of light,
My home is there, my home is there.

2 Where living fountains sweetly flow,
Where buds and flowers immortal grow,
Where trees their fruits celestial bear,
My home is there, my home is there.

3 Away from sorrow, doubt and pain,
Away from worldly loss and gain,
From all temptation, tears and care,
My home is there, my home is there.

4 Beyond the bright and pearly gate,
Where Jesus, loving Saviour, waits,
Where all is peaceful, bright and fair,
My home is there, my home is there.

81. Gathering Home.

Music No. 162 in "Precious Hymns."

Up to the bountiful giver of life,—
  Gathering home! gathering home!
Up to the dwelling where cometh no strife,
  The dear ones are gathering home.

Cho.—Gathering home! gathering home!
  Never to sorrow more, never to roam;
Gathering home! gathering home!
  God's children are gathering home.

2 Up to the city where falleth no night,—
  Gathering home! gathering home!
Up where the Saviour's own face is the light,
  The dear ones are gathering home.

3 Up to the beautiful mansions above,—
  Gathering home! gathering home!
Safe in the arms of his infinite love,
  The dear ones are gathering home.
        MARIANA B. SLADE.

82. Home of the Soul.

I WILL sing you a song of a beautiful land,
  The far-away home of the soul,
Where no storms ever beat on the glittering strand
  While the years of eternity roll.

2 Oh, that home of the soul, in my visions and dreams
  Its bright jasper walls I can see;
Till I fancy but thinly the vail intervenes
  Between that fair city and me.

3 That unchangeable home is for you and for me,
  Where Jesus of Nazareth stands;
The King of all kingdoms forever is he,
  And he holdeth our crowns in his hands.

4 Oh, how sweet it will be in that beautiful land,
  So free from all sorrow and pain,
With songs on our lips, and with harps in our hands,
  To meet one another again!

83. The Bleeding Lamb.

From "The Quiver." Tune, p. 10

My Saviour suffered on the tree
  Glory to the bleeding Lamb;
Oh, come and view the Lord v
  Glory to the bleeding Lamb!

Cho.—The Lamb! the Lamb!
  bleeding Lamb!
I love the sound of Jesus' nam
  It sets my spirit all aflame,
Glory to the bleeding Lamb!

2 He bore my sins, and curse,
    shame,
  And I am saved through Je
    name,

3 I know my sins are all forgive
  And I am on my way to heaven

4 And when the storms of life
  I'll sing upon a happier shore.
    o'er.

5 And this my ceaseless song
    be,—
  That Jesus tasted death for n

84. The New Song.

Music No. 8 in "Precious Hymn

THERE are songs of joy that I k
    to sing,
  When my heart was as blithe
    bird in spring!
But the song I have learned
    full of cheer
That the dawn shines out in
    darkness drear.

Cho.—O the new, new song!
  new, new song!
I can sing it now with the rans
    throng:
Power and dominion to him
    shall reign,
Glory and praise to the Lamb
    was slain.

2 There are strains of home that
    dear as life,
  And I list to them oft 'mid th
    of strife;
But I know of a home that is
    drous fair,
And I sing the psalm they are
    ing there.
        FLORA L.

85 The Blood's Applied.

Music No. 52 in "Songs of Perfect Love."

The blood's applied! my soul is free,
I'm saved, without, within;
The blood of Jesus cleanseth me
From every trace of sin.

Cho.—The blood's applied, I'm justified,
It pardons every sin;
The blood's applied, I'm sanctified,
It makes me pure within.

2 I've bid farewell to every fear,
By faith I claim the prize;
Now I can read my title clear
To mansions in the skies.

3 Temptations come, and trials, too;
While hellish darts are hurled;
But Jesus saves me through and through,
In spite of all the world.

4 Let cares and storms and trials fall
About me thick and fast,
My Jesus, he is Lord of all,
Will bring me home at last.

5 Then will my happy, happy soul
Sing of his love and rest,
While shouts of victory shall roll
From every conquering breast.

86 Sunshine in the Soul.

Music No. 146 in "Precious Hymns."

There's sunshine in my soul to-day,
More glorious and bright
Than glows in any earthly sky,
For Jesus is my light.

Ref.—Oh, there's sunshine, blessed sunshine,
When the peaceful, happy moments roll;
When Jesus shows his smiling face
There is sunshine in the soul.

2 There's music in my soul to-day,
A carol to my King,
And Jesus, listening, can hear
The songs I cannot sing.

3 There's springtime in my soul to-day,
For when the Lord is near,
The dove of peace sings in my heart,
The flowers of grace appear.

4 There's gladness in my soul to-day,
And hope, and praise, and love,
For blessing which he gives me now,
For joys "laid up" above.

87 Entire Consecration.

Music No. 94 in "Precious Hymns."

Take my life, and let it be
Consecrated, Lord, to thee;
Take my hands, and let them move
At the impulse of thy love.

2 Take my feet, and let them be
Swift and beautiful for thee;
Take my voice, and let me sing
Always, only, for my King.

3 Take my lips, and let them be
Filled with messages for thee;
Take my silver and my gold,—
Not a mite would I withhold.

4 Take my moments, and my days,
Let them flow in endless praise;
Take my intellect, and use
Every power as thou shalt choose.

5 Take my will, and make it thine;
It shall be no longer mine;
Take my heart,—it is thine own,—
It shall be thy royal throne.

88 Hallelujah, Amen!

One day, as I was walking
Along the lonesome road,
My heart was filled with rapture,—
I heard the voice of God.

Cho.—Hallelujah, amen! hallelujah, amen!
Hallelujah, amen! amen! amen!

2 He chose me for his watchman
To stand on Zion's wall,
Saying, Go and preach my Gospel,
Glad tidings unto all.

3 The cross is great and heavy,
And I am in my youth;
I'm 'fraid I am not able
To preach the Word of Truth.

4 Says Jesus, "Lo! I'm with you,"
In every trying hour;
And though you are deficient,
I am the God of power.

5 I took the Gospel trumpet,
And I began to blow;
And if my Lord will help me,
I'll preach where'er I go.

6 And when my mission's ended,
I'll blow the trump no more;
I'll join my fellow-watchmen
On Canaan's happy shore.

89. Jesus is Good to Me.

Music No. 107 in "Precious Hymns."

I LOVE my Saviour, his heart is good,
He has loved me o'er and o'er;
He sought me when wan'dring, I'm saved by his blood.
And I love him more and more.

CHO.—||:Jesus is good to me::||
So good! so good!
Jesus is good to my soul.

2 He calls, I rise, he maketh me whole,—
How fond his tender embrace!
He cleanses, keeps, and blesses my soul,—
My day the smile of his face.

3 I want to love him with all my heart,
Though all its powers are small;
I will not keep him from any part,
For he is worthy of all.

4 He's good to me in my sorrow's night,
He's good in the tempest's roll;
He bringeth from darkness into light,—
With joy he filleth my soul.

90. We Are More Than Conquerors.

Music No. 191 in "The Quartet."

WHAT shall separate us
From the love that bought us?
Shall the pangs of anguish
Which the cross has wrought us?
Doubtings and distresses,
Fiery trials prove us;
Yet am I persuaded
None of these shall move us.

CHO.—We are more than conquerors,
More, yea, more::||
||:We are more than conquerors,:||
Through him that loved us.

2 Things to come or present,
Whatsoe'er betide us,—
Life nor death shall ever
From our Lord divide us.
Angels, powers, dominions,
These shall fall before us;
Clothed in his salvation,
With his banner o'er us.

91. None Like Jesus.

Music No. 6 in "Glad Hallelujah."

WE love to tell of him who came
Our gentle guide to be
Though earthly friends around us
There's none so dear as he. [cling

CHO.—None like Jesus, Hallelujah,
None so dear as he;
Though earthly friends around us cling,
There's none so dear as he.

2 We love to seek his promised grace,
And ask his tender care;
We love to hear his precious name,
And breathe that name in prayer.

3 We love to know that day by day
We do not walk alone,
If one in him our faith can feel
His hand within our own.

4 O, may he lead us safely on
Till days and years are past;
Then take our happy souls on high
To dwell with him at last.

92. I'm Happy, so Happy.

Music No. 30 in "Sunlit Songs."

I'M happy, so happy! no words can express
The joy and the comfort I see,
For Jesus hath purchased, thro' infinite grace,
A perfect salvation for me.

CHO.—Saved, saved, oh, glory to God!
I feel the assurance divine;
Saved, saved, oh, glory to God!
His spirit bears witness with mine.

2 I'm happy, so happy! while trusting in him,
Whose presence o'ershadows my way;
Who leadeth my soul by the river of peace,
And giveth me strength as my day.

3 My love may be tested, my faith may be tried
The depth of its fervor to prove,
But welcome each trial, my Saviour designs
The gold from the dross to remove,

93 The Blood Washed Pilgrim.

Music No. 152 in "Songs of Perfect Love."

I saw a blood-washed pilgrim,
 A sinner saved by grace,
Upon the King's great highway,
 With peaceful, shining face.
Temptations sore beset him,
 But nothing could affright;
He said, "The yoke is easy,
 The burden, it is light."

Cho.—Oh, palms of victory, crowns of glory,
 Palms of victory I shall wear.

2 His helmet was salvation,
 A simple faith his shield,
And righteousness his breast-plate;
 The Spirit's sword he'd wield.
All fiery darts arrested
 And quenched their blazing flight;
He cried, "The yoke is easy,
 The burden, it is light."

3 I saw him in the furnace,
 He doubted not, nor feared,
And in the flames beside him
 The Son of God appeared.
Though seven times 'twas heated
 With all the tempter's might,
He said "The yoke is easy,
 The burden, it is light."

4 'Mid storms, and clouds, and trials,
 In prison, at the stake,
He leaped for joy, rejoicing,
 'Twas all for Jesus' sake.
That God should count him worthy,
 Was such supreme delight,
He cried, "The yoke is easy,
 The burden is so light."

5 I saw him overcoming
 Through all the swelling strife,
Until he crossed the threshold
 Of God's Eternal Life.
The Crown, the Throne, the Sceptre,
 The Name, the Stone so White,
Were his, who found, in Jesus,
 The yoke and burden light.

94 Keep Close to Jesus.

Music No. 271 in "Unfading Treasures."

When you start for the land of heavenly rest,
 Keep close to Jesus all the way;
For he is the Guide, and he knows the way best,
 Keep close to Jesus all the way.

Cho.—||: Keep close to Jesus, :||
 Keep close to Jesus all the way;
By day or by night, never turn from the right,
 Keep close to Jesus all the way.

2 Never mind the storms or trials as you go,
 Keep close to Jesus all the way;
'Tis a comfort and joy his favor to know;
 Keep close to Jesus all the way.

3 To be safe from the darts of the evil one,
 Keep close to Jesus all the way;
Take the shield of faith till the victory is won;
 Keep close to Jesus all the way.

4 We shall reach our home in heaven by and bye;
 Keep close to Jesus all the way;
Where to those we love we'll never say good-bye,
 Keep close to Jesus all the way.
 —John Lane.

95 Jesus Comes.

Music No. 95 in "The Quartet."

Watch, ye saints, with eyelids waking,
Lo, the pow'rs of heav'n are shaking,
Keep your lamps all trimm'd and burning,
Ready for your Lord's returning.

Cho.—Lo! he comes, lo! Jesus comes;
Lo! he comes, he comes all glorious!
Jesus comes to reign victorious,
Lo! he comes, yes, Jesus comes.

2 Lo! the promise of your Saviour,
Pardoned sin and purchased favor,
Blood-washed robes and crowns of glory;
Haste to tell redemption's story.

3 Kingdoms at their base are crumbling,
Hark, his chariot wheels are rumbling,
Tell, oh, tell of grace abounding,
Whilst the seventh trump is sounding.

4 Nations wane, though proud and stately,
Christ his kingdom hasteneth greatly,
Earth her latest pangs is summing,
Shout, ye saints, your Lord is coming.

97   Shall I Turn Back? *(Copyright.)*

1 LOST, lost on the mountains of sin
    and despair,
Till Jesus in love sought and res-
    cued me there,
He saved me from wand'ring, he
    gave me release,
And led me to pathways of blessing
    and peace.

CHO.—And shall I turn back into the
    world?
    Oh, no! not I! not I!
    And shall I turn back into the
    world?
    No, no, not I!

2 My days, swiftly passing, have
    brought from above
So many bright tokens of mercy
    and love;
"More grace" he has given, and
    burdens removed,
Yes, over and over, his goodness
    I've proved.

3 How well I remember, in sorrow's
    dark night,
The lamp of his word shed its beau-
    tiful light,
And sweet was the voice of the
    Comforter then,
Awaking new praises again and
    again.

4 Before me the tow'rs of Jerusalem
    rise,
Each day I am nearing my home in
    the skies;
My Savior a mansion of joy will
    prepare,
And loved ones are waiting to wel-
    come me there.
                      —E. E. Hewitt.

98   Fill Me Now. *(Copyright.)*

HOVER o'er me, Holy Spirit;
    Bathe my trembling heart and brow;
Fill me with thy hallow'd presence,
    Come, oh, come and fill me now.

CHO.—Fill me now, fill me now,
    Jesus, come, and fill me now;
Fill me with thy hallow'd presence,—
    Come, oh, come and fill me now.

2 Thou canst fill me, gracious Spirit,
    Though I cannot tell thee how;
But I need thee, greatly need thee,
    Come, oh, come and fill me now.

3 I am weakness, full of weakness;
    At thy sacred feet I bow;
Blest, divine, eternal Spirit,
    Fill with power, and fill me now.

4 Cleanse and comfort; bless and save
    me;
    Bathe, oh, bathe my heart and brow!
Thou art comforting and saving,
    Thou art sweetly filling now.
                 —Rev. E. H. Stokes, D.D.

99   Beulah Land. *(Copyright.)*

I'VE reached the land of corn and wine,
And all its riches freely mine;
Here shines undimmed one blissful day,
For all my night has passed away.

CHO.—O Beulah Land, sweet Beulah
    Land,
As on thy highest mount I stand,
I look away across the sea,
Where mansions are prepared for me,
And view the shining glory shore,—
My heaven, my home for evermore!

2 My Saviour comes and walks with me,
And sweet communion here have we;
He gently leads me by his hand,
For this is heaven's border-land.

3 A sweet perfume upon the breeze
Is borne from ever-vernal trees,
And flowers, that never-fading grow
Where streams of life forever flow.

4 The zephyrs seem to float to me
Sweet sounds of heaven's melody,
As angels with the white-robed throng
Join in the sweet redemption song.
                       —Edgar Page.

100   More About Jesus. *(Copyright.)*

MORE about Jesus would I know,
More of his grace to others show;
More of his saving fulness see,
More of his love who died for me.

CHO.—More, more about Jesus,
    More, more about Jesus;
More of his saving fulness see,
    More of his love who died for me

2 More about Jesus let me learn,
More of his holy will discern;
Spirit of God, my teacher be,
Showing the things of Christ to me.

3 More about Jesus; in his word,
Holding communion with my Lord;
Hearing his voice in every line,
Making each faithful saying mine.

4 More about Jesus; on his throne,
Riches in glory all his own;
More of his kingdom's sure increase;
More of his coming, Prince of Peace.
                       —E. E. Hewitt.

I've Found the Canaan Land. 101

C. H. M.
Mrs. C. H. Morris.

1. I've found the "Canaan land" of promise, With joys akin to those above;
2. I've found the blessed "Rock of Ages," And 'neath its shadow stretching wide,
3. I've found the gem of full salvation, The precious "Pearl of greatest price;"

At God's command I've cross'd "clean over" In- to the land of "perfect love."
Although the tempest 'round me rages, In peace and safety I a-bide.
I'm sav'd from sin and condemnation, Thro' Christ the bleeding sacrifice.

CHORUS.

I'm dwelling in the land of Beu-lah, I'm o-ver on the vic-t'ry side;
I'm singing glo-ry, hal-le-lu-jah! Ho-san-na to the Cru-ci-fied.
I'm singing glo-ry, hal-le-lu-jah! Ho-sanna to the Cru-ci-fied.

Copyright, 1899, by John J. Hood.

4 I've found the "well of living water,"
The balm for sin and earthly strife;
Within my heart 'tis ever springing
Up into everlasting life.

5 I've found a feast of "hidden manna,"
And strength for every time and place;
There's in my heart a glad hosanna
To him who saves me by his grace.

Life's Railway to Heaven.—CONCLUDED. 103

Where the an-gels wait to join us In thy praise for-ev-ermore.

Jesus Brought me Back.

C. J. B.   CHAS. J. BUTLER.

1. Far from Christ I wandered, Sought for rest in vain, Till the loving
2. When I un-to Sa-tan Lent a list'n-ing ear, Soon my feet were
3. Mine was bit-ter anguish While from Christ a-stray, But since me he
4. In the ear of Je-sus Oft I breathe my pray'r, That he'd ev-er

CHORUS.

Shepherd   Brought me back again.   I'm so glad Christ found me, And
straying   In the desert drear.
res-cued   Joy-ous is the day.
keep me   In his tender care.

brought me to his fold; Oh, joy he gave me Nev-er can be told.

Copyright, 1879, by J. Hood.

104 Jesus Leads.

"And when he putteth forth his own sheep, he goeth before them, and the sheep follow him: for they know his voice."—John x: 4.

JOHN R. CLEMENTS.
JNO. R. SWENEY.

Andante.

1. Like a shepherd, tender, true, Jesus leads, . . . Jesus leads, . .
2. All a-long life's rugged road Jesus leads, . . . Jesus leads, . .
3. Thro' the sun-lit ways of life Jesus leads, . . . Jesus leads, . .

Daily finds us pastures new, Jesus leads, . . . Jesus leads; . .
Till we reach yon blest a-bode, Jesus leads, . . . Jesus leads; . .
Thro' the warings and the strife Jesus leads, . . . Jesus leads; . .

If thick mists are o'er the way, . . Or the flock 'mid danger feeds, . .
All the way, before, he's trod, . And he now . . the flock precedes, . .
When we reach . the Jordan's tide, Where life's bound-'ry-line re-cedes, . .

He will watch them lest they stray, Jesus leads, . . Jesus leads.
Safe in-to the fold of God Jesus leads, . . Jesus leads.
He will spread the waves a-side, Jesus leads, . . Jesus leads.

Copyright, 1895, by Jno. R. Sweney.

A Sinner Saved.—CONCLUDED. 107

And I'll tell forev er How he saved when I came pleading before his feet.

Neither Do I Condemn Thee.

F. M. D.   "Go, and sin no more."—John viii: 11.   FRANK M. DAVIS.

1. Penitent, sin-confessing One, to Jesus came, Looking to him for pardon,
2. Never a trembling sinner, Bowing at his feet, Seeking the promis'd blessing
3. Ye that are heavy laden, Burden'd with your sin, Jesus will now relieve you,

Trusting in his name; Je-sus in tones of pit-y Spake as ne'er before,
At the mercy seat, Ever has heard but welcome, Welcome o'er and o'er;
Kindly take you in; Sweetly he bids you enter At the o-pen door;

CHORUS.

"Neither do I condemn thee, Go, and sin no more." "Go, and sin no more,

Go, and sin no more; Neither do I condemn thee, Go, and sin no more."

From "Brightest Glory." By per. of John J. Hood.

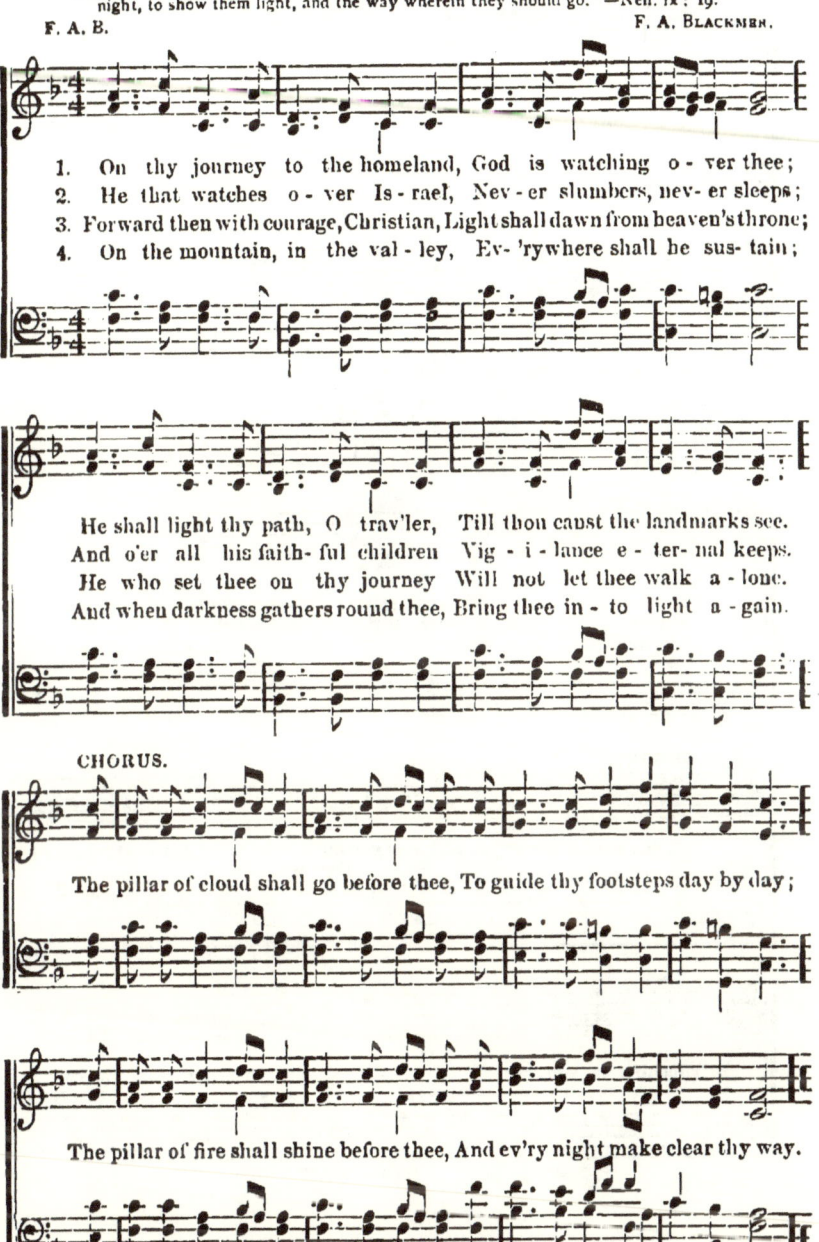

114. Sunshine As You Go.

John M. Baker.   Jno. R. Sweney.

Moderato.

1. Oh, the world has need of sunshine as you go, For we oft-en see the tears of sor-row flow; You can haste that com-ing day, When they'll all be wiped away, If you scatter blessed sunshine as you go.
2. You can la-bor for the Master as you go, Plant the precious seed and he will bid it grow; Toil-ing on, whate'er betide, With the Saviour by your side, You can scatter blessed sunshine as you go.
3. You will meet with many trials as you go, There will be some self-de-ni-als here be-low; But keep look-ing still above, And re-member God is love, While you scatter blessed sunshine as you go.

CHORUS.

You can scatter blessed sunshine as you go, ... You can scatter blessed blessed sunshine as you go, sunshine as you go; bless-ed sunshine as you go; Oh, so many hearts are sad, You can

Copyright, 1897, by Jno. R. Sweney.

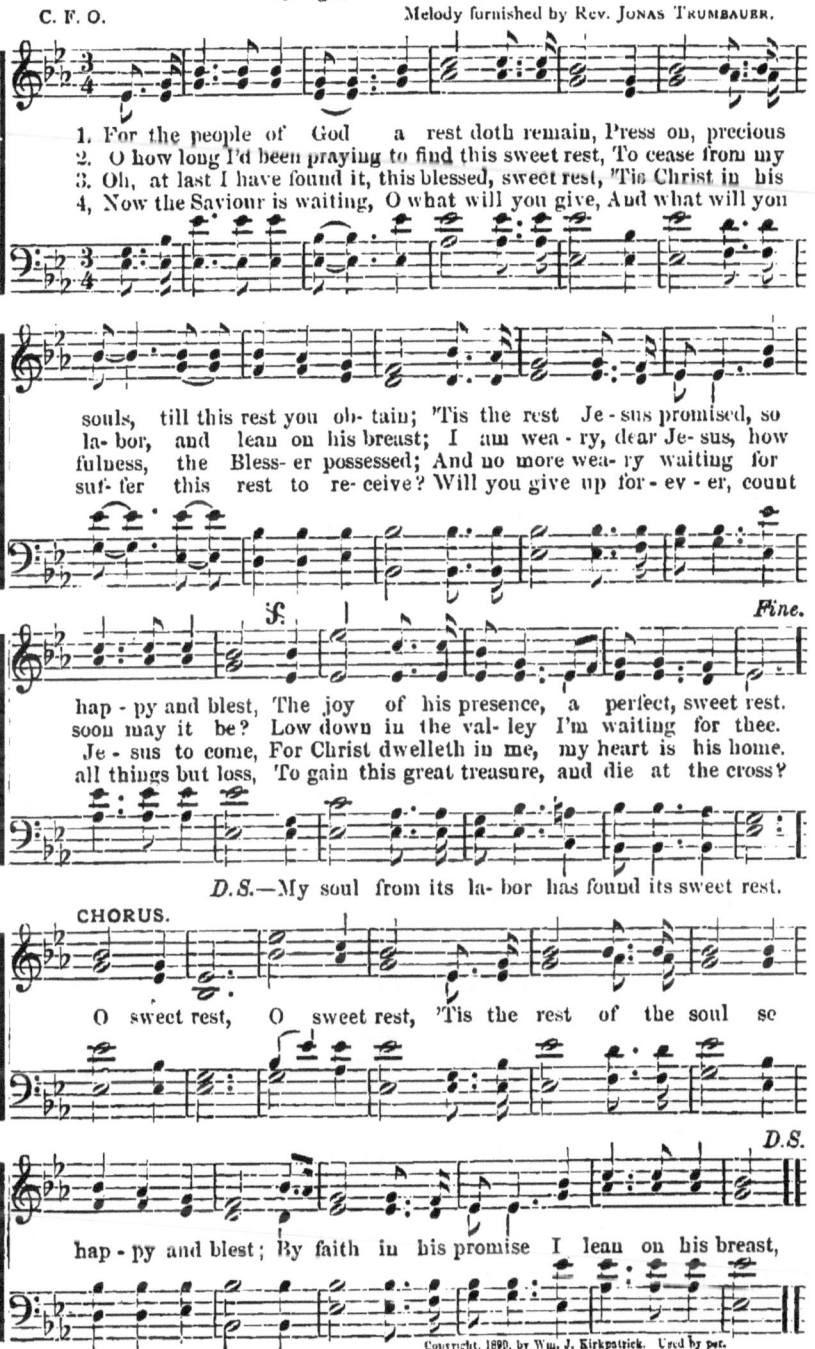

On to Victory.—CONCLUDED.

Onward in the conflict, hop-ing, trusting, On to vic-to-ry!

Be of Good Cheer.

CHARLOTTE ABBEY. "Be of good cheer: It is I; be not afraid."—Mark vi: 60. FRANK M. DAVIS.

1. "Be of good cheer," saith the Saviour, "Tho' all thy brightest hopes fade;
2. "Be of good cheer, tho' the tempter And world are 'gainst thee array'd;
3. "Be of good cheer thro' thy tri-als; On me let burdens be laid;

I will be near to sus-tain thee; It is I, O be not a-fraid."
I will give grace that will conquer; It is I, O be not a-fraid."
Tho' they be heavy, I'll bear them; It is I, O be not a-fraid."

CHORUS.

It is I, ... it is I, ... It is I, O be not a-fraid!
 It is I, it is I,

"Be of good cheer," saith the Saviour; "It is I, O be not a-fraid!"

From "Notes of Praise." By per. of John J. Hood.

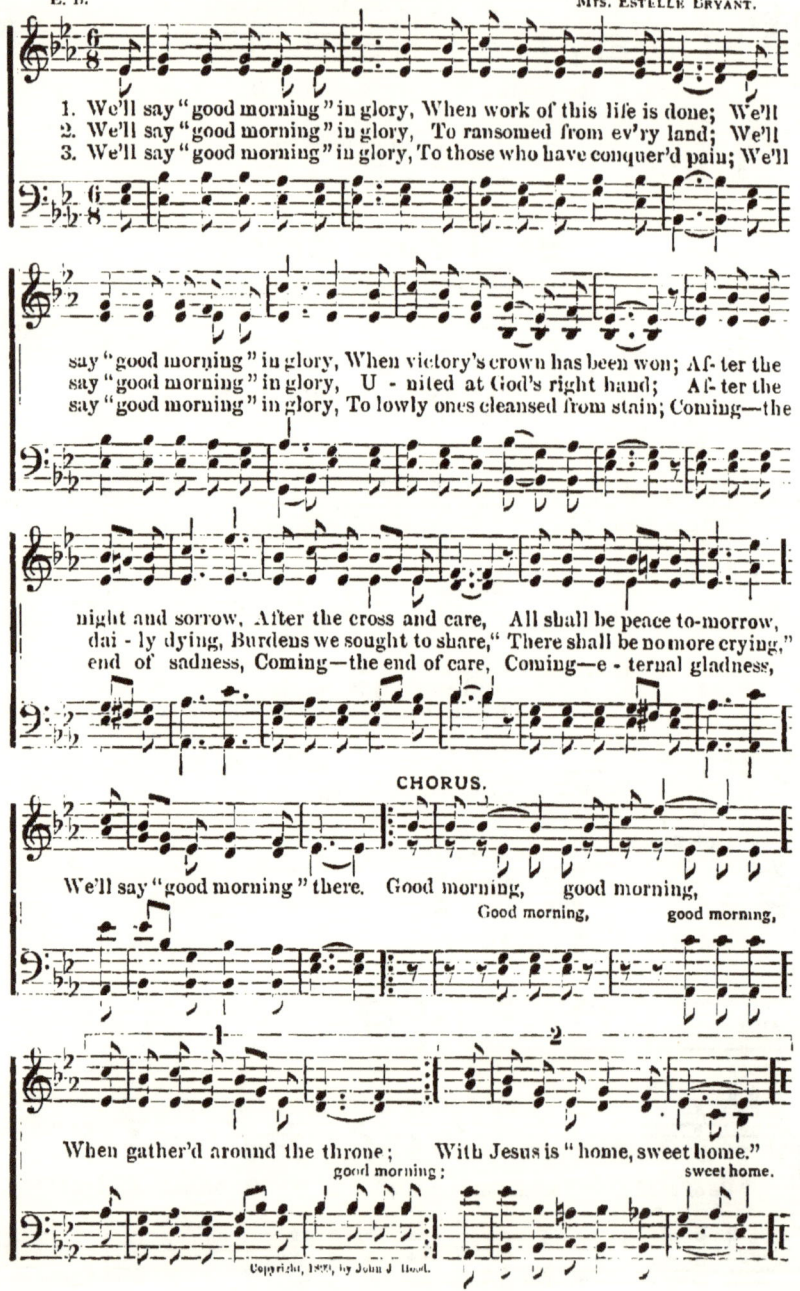

4 It brings a message full of love,
  Hallelujah! grace is free!
  A message from the throne above,
  Hallelujah! grace is free!
  The Spirit now invites you, "come!"
  The Saviour calls, "no longer roam!"
  The Father pleads, "my child, come
  Hallelujah! grace is free! [home!"

5 The conflict o'er, at God's right hand,
  Hallelujah! grace is free!
  Redeemed from every race and land,
  Hallelujah! grace is free!
  We shall behold him face to face,
  And sing the wonders of his grace
  Who died to save our sinful race,
  Hallelujah! grace is free!

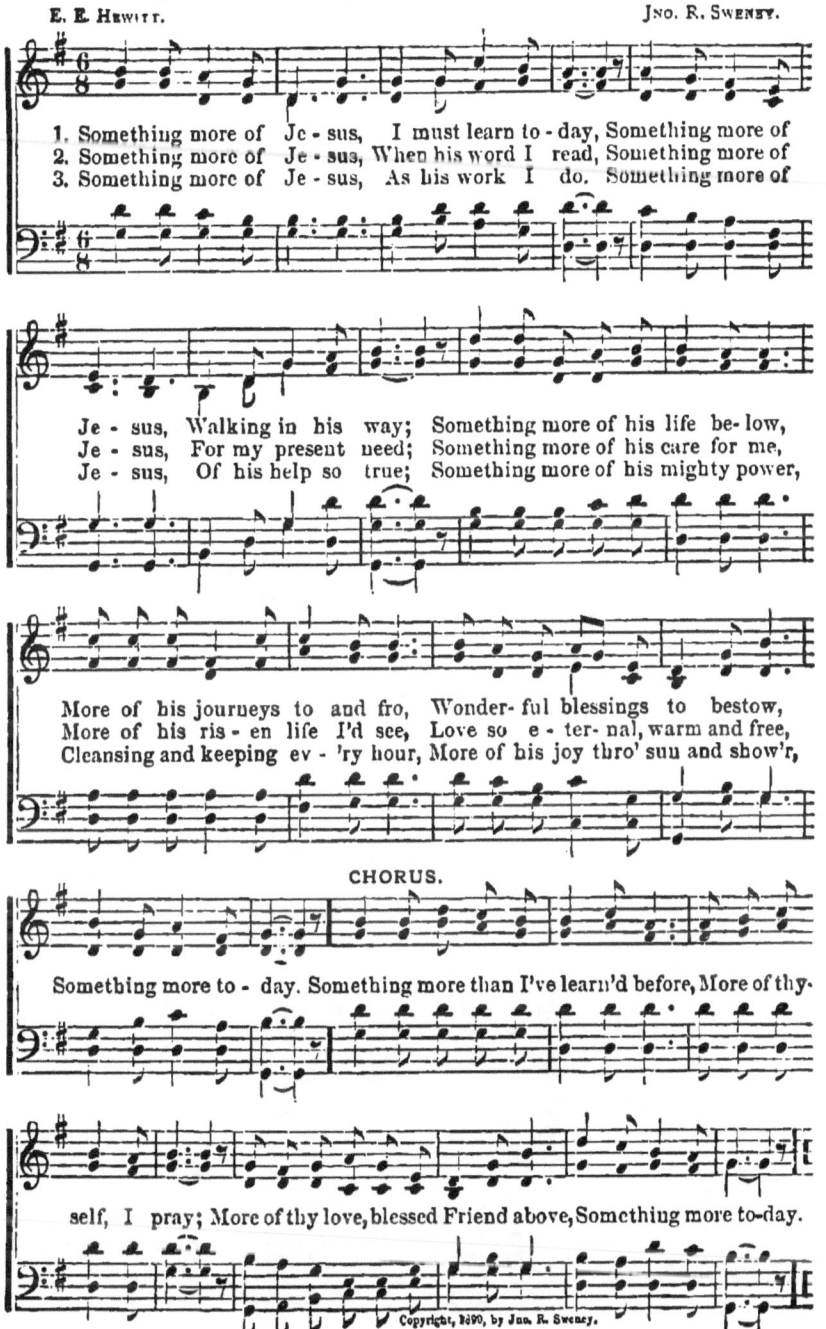

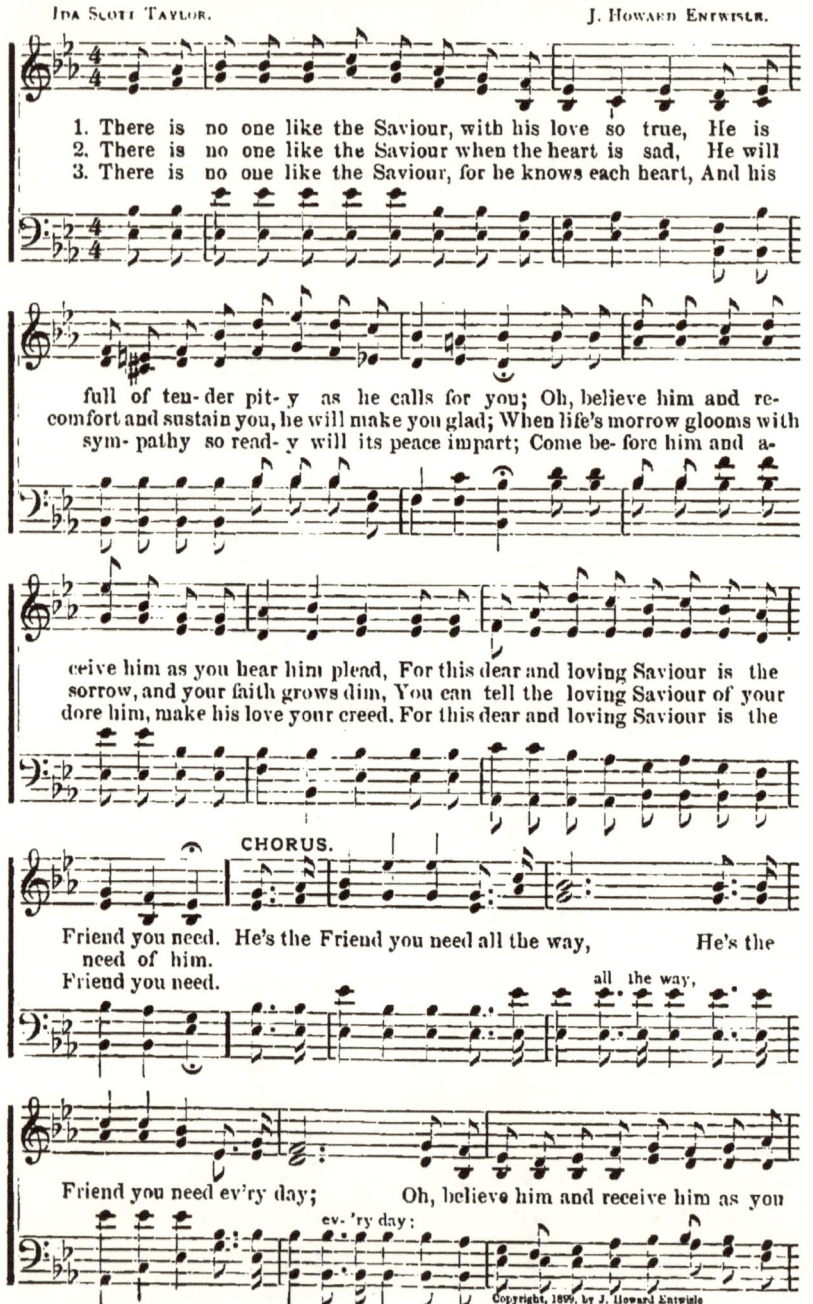

www.ingramcontent.com/pod-product-compliance
Lightning Source LLC
Chambersburg PA
CBHW020331090426
42735CB00009B/1494